MW01132958

SHORTCUTS

better ways to better days

(Truisms, Life Lessons, Adult Skills, and Humor)

MARK LUNDHOLM

Illustrations by Kyle Spencer

wholehearted
PUBLISHING

Published by Wholehearted Publishing
Sacramento, California

www.wholeheartedpublishing.com

ISBN: 978-1-7345238-4-3

1st printing

Cover and Interior Design: Kyle Spencer, Bernadette Robancho, AJ Foxx
Illustrations: Kyle Spencer

Table of Contents

Introduction

This book, one of the most painstaking and gratifying creative efforts I have ever attempted, is the result of years of tears, trials and errors, triumphs and terrors, and . . . lessons learned the hard way: by making costly mistakes.

I titled this book *Shortcuts* for that very reason.

One of the most important jobs a generation of human beings has is to pass on what they know, learn, and experience so that the next generation and every generation to follow won't have to make the same mistakes, the same incorrect guesses, or spend valuable time trying to figure out everything on their own.

What you are about to read is absolutely full of that stuff!

A note of caution here, though. If you are extremely fragile or fractured easily when it comes to words, STOP READING NOW. You may not survive the encounter. The truth is sometimes hard to digest because, initially, it may be uncomfortable to receive. My experience is that "comfortable" is not the ally of people who want to grow into the best version of themselves. So buckle up those seat belts, stow your tray tables, and adjust your chairs to the most straight-up and uncomfortable position. You are taking a trip, departing from where you are comfortable now. The trip will become turbulent, strange, awkward, and unusually bumpy, but sometimes that's exactly the ride we need to take us from average to exceptional, from here to heroic, from now to WOW!!! I'm not judgin', I'm just sayin'.

If you mention the word "shortcut," people generally fall into one of two camps.

Camp one consists of those who think of a shortcut as taking the easy way out, as permission to make less than 100 percent effort; an unproductive, unfinished, lazy work ethic. Camp two consists of those who see a shortcut as the more direct route, an efficient way to save some time, the "been there, learned that" kind of folks.

I have been in both camps. I prefer the latter. A shortcut can be the best way to get to a better place. It is a simpler path toward doing something, being something, learning something, seeing something, healing something, feeling something valuable, vital, exciting, inviting, authentic, and important.

Life is a long road, and human beings are flawed. The tools, information, and life skills presented in this book are not. That statement may seem arrogant or accurate depending on who you are, what you believe, where you have been in your life, and why you're still reading. Finish the book, and I'll live with your decision. You won't be wrong. You'll be certain.

Each chapter begins with a shortcut—a simple and solid suggestion—followed by a brief description of that shortcut, then stories that illustrate how that shortcut was either ignored or used, followed or found, depending on the time and stage of my development as a human being.

There is a question or two at the end of each chapter: a "reflection section" just for you.

This book is my gift to you as we share the load on this road. You are not alone.

Enjoy the work,

Chapter 1

First Thought Wrong

This is a personal, painful, sometimes comical condition I have had since I can remember. I cannot say for sure whether it is clinical or chemical, nature or nurture, because I'm not a physician, clinician, or mental health expert. I just know it is very real.

FTW: first thought wrong. Wrong answer, wrong direction, reaction or response, or interpretation. These include inaccurate, incorrect, impolite, ungrateful, judgmental, sarcastic, abusive, evasive, dishonest, misguided, egotistical thoughts that always lead to . . . "Oops! Well, that isn't gonna work."

It's like a laser-guided missile system. FTW is the laser, and its focus is the target. Once the target is painted, the missile hits where it is AIMED. . . and BOOM! Then whatever was injured or destroyed needs to be repaired or rebuilt.

On any given day, our first twenty thoughts can be wrong, long, and strong. For me, healthy thoughts DO show up eventually. But they are NEVER the first one.

THE UNMASKED BANDIT

Way back in the 1980s, during my alcohol-fueled cocaine-crazy twenties, I robbed a liquor store in San Leandro, California. (I don't usually tell this story when I'm doing a corporate motivational gig, by the way.) So here's how it went down:

I used to like to tell people that I was a cocaine dealer. Truth is . . . I was a cocaine user. If I had dealt it instead of snorting it, I'd have had a house or two and a car or three and a whole bunch of money stacked in a bank somewhere. Yup, I was a user. And every cocaine dealer knows that users are losers. I've never met an active drug user with an effective retirement strategy or an attractive financial portfolio. No drug user quits because they're on a winning streak.

From time to time, I would run out of money. Eventually, I would have to squeak out some kind of sideways coke deal, make some money playing poker, or steal it. It's funny how money never just showed up when I needed it. When I was way, way down financially, it always seemed to feed me creatively. Drugs, alcohol, money, crime, loss, drugs, alcohol, money, crime, loss, repeat. A sadistic cycle that did nothing but flip me over and over like a sock in the dryer. But for some reason, during that period of my life, I could always find a way to get the money to continue the cycle. I probably thought it was a talent back then. Ahh, youth!

A guy I knew worked at a liquor store. He made the mistake of telling me that they kept the big money (the fifties and hundreds) in a cigar box under some brown bags, two shelves below the cash register on the counter. First thought? Rob that liquor store. No regard or thoughts for my safety or possible consequences. And even less concern for my friend. That's how I treated most of my friends back then. That's just the way it was. Street dope people don't really have friends or acquaintances. They have accessories and sometimes willing (or unwitting) accomplices.

So one Friday night, I put my plan together. My tools were these: a pale blue Derby jacket, black jeans, and a black ski mask. I put all these tools under the front seat of a stolen pickup truck and carefully drove to the liquor store.

As I got behind the wheel, I examined my secret weapon: a bottle of Oxy-5 acne medicine. When pressed against the lining of the inside of the Derby jacket pocket, the lid of the bottle looked like the snub-nosed barrel of

a gun. Of course, I didn't have a real gun . . . but I did have acne at the time. Pretty good plan, huh?

I waited until almost closing time. I looked in through the front window of the liquor store, and I pushed the top of the bottle up against the pocket of the jacket, pretending I had a gun. I prepared to pull the ski mask down over my face.

Question here: Why is this thing called a ski mask? How many times have you seen anyone skiing in one of these things? No! This is an armed robbery mask!

So . . . I'm running into the liquor store. Pumped up . . . Determined . . . Driven . . . Forceful . . . And I pulled the mask down wrong! My right eye was showing out of the left eye hole. The right eye hole exposed my right ear, and the mouth hole was on my neck! So I could only see half the store, but I could hear fairly well.

I yelled at the clerk (NOT anyone I knew), "Hsjsuebbeiubsggysvv!"

He looked at me, annoyed, and said, "What?" So I pulled the mouth hole from the side of my neck to expose my top lip and my entire nose. I said, "Get your face down on that damn floor!" He did.

As I went to the register, trying to find the right button, I watched the clerk and checked the front door, all with one eye. The Oxy-5 bottle started to leak through the front of the pocket.

This plan was starting to look like a bad idea. I opened the register's cash drawer, grabbed the money, and ran out of the liquor store. I didn't stop running until I was sure I hadn't been followed and I could sit down somewhere hidden and safe to catch my breath.

Now, there are always three reactions when I tell that story.

Reaction number one: You could've been killed! Nobody knew for sure it wasn't a real gun. What if they shot you?!

Reaction number two: Dude, what about the cigar box? (I forgot all about it.)

And reaction number three: (from the serious alcoholics) You didn't even grab a BOTTLE on the way out? What are you, new?

From my very first thought about that liquor store, I added several more wrong, narrow, short-sighted, and greedy thoughts without slowing down. First thought wrong can also be long and strong, and it could have cost me a lot more than embarrassment, panic, and a shaky walk home that night.

INSIDE SAN QUENTIN

My first real-life comedy performance was a fifteen-minute set I had written to be performed in San Quentin (SQ) State penitentiary. I was probably around sixty-five days sober and living in a halfway house in San Leandro, California. I had become part of a performance troupe called Act 12. We were a motley crew of recovering people who had a large (or limited) amount of talent to share with what we thought would be great venues of receptive individuals for a message of hope, healing, and sobriety. It was a mixed bag of musicians, actors, orators, artists, poets, a master of ceremonies, and ONE comedian.

I had auditioned a couple of weeks before the SQ show; I was the only individual to audition for the comedy slot. I'm sure I was funny, but looking back, I may have gotten the part by attrition. All I know is that I wanted to give something back. Back to the community I had survived.

On the afternoon of the show, our MC, René Rodriguez, informed me that I would be going on first. First! Remember the scene in Saving Private Ryan where the troop carriers are lowering their doors to send the soldiers out onto the beach from the watercraft? Remember the guys who caught a bullet right in their hel-

meted forehead? Before the door was even halfway down? Well . . . that was about to be me.

I wrote out my best comedy set and prepared for the worst experience. I had been preparing for this show my whole life, yet I've always been a pessimist because that way I'm never disappointed.

I stood off to the side of the stage and listened to René say, "Please welcome to the stage, our funniest performer, Comedian Mark L." There was a smattering of polite applause, and I traded places with the MC.

René stood off to the side and watched me as I grabbed the microphone with both hands and started to tremble. The words I had written, memorized, and rehearsed stumbled out of my mouth, and I barely recognized them myself. I'm sure the audience also struggled with my pronunciations, delivery, and timing, three of the most important things in comedy. The entire place knew it was my first time. They could smell it. This was not a crowd that got fooled very often. Certainly not tonight. My first thought? ATTACK! Show them I'm in charge! Puff myself up and charge!

As I looked out over the crowd, I noticed how separated they were. The Latinos were in the back left corner. The Asians were in the front right section. African Americans were in the front left section, and the white Aryan nation took up the back right corner. It was like the board game Sorry with four different colors.

Up on the railing on the gymnasium's second floor was a correctional officer with a shotgun. He was keeping an eye on the entire group . . . Including me. I was standing behind an eight-foot-high cyclone fence that separated the stage from the front row.

As I looked out at the audience, I noticed one singularly unique human being. He was in front of the front row, by himself, staring at me as though I was a lambchop and he hadn't eaten since middle school. He was massive! Huge, ripped, buff, cut, musclebound. He had muscles in his eyes! He had a bald head and wore a tank top and state-issued jeans. From the bottom of his chin to what I'm sure were the tips of his toes, he was covered in prison tattoos. Covered. And he was staring at me.

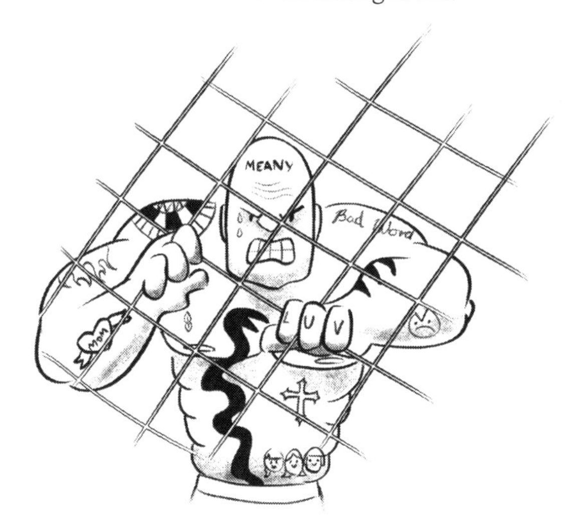

I panicked and said," Look at you, tough guy. Smooth head, all that ink. You could be a ballpoint pen!" No one laughed.

On the upper railing, I heard the officer rack his shotgun: chk-chk!

The convict lifted his massive frame out of his chair, walked up to the stage, stuck his fingers through the fence—huge ham-hock-sized hands with fingers the size of bratwurst—and in a low, brutal voice said, "Hey, funny man, I've got friends on the outside. They will find you, tie you to a tree in your yard, and burn your house to the ground."

I remember thinking to myself: THIS is a heckler! Some drunken fella in a comedy club? Wants to talk about my mother? Bring it on! I've still got my house and my rear end.

I looked over to René, my eyes pleading with him to pull me off the stage and bring on the next act. Instead, he folded his arms across his chest and slowly shook his head from side to side. I was two minutes into my set with thirteen minutes to go, and he was going to make sure that I did my entire time. I had created this situation, and no one was coming to rescue me. I was responsible for what was happening to me, and I was gonna learn something from the situation, even if I hated the experience. It was a lot like my drinking and using career.

I've been challenged on stage hundreds of times since performing in SQ. While my first thought is always "Take 'em on" or "shut 'em down" or "show 'em who's running the show," I learned in San Quentin to assess the surroundings, check the threat level, think about what's coming next, and then proceed with the ha-ha that best serves the comedy process. It's a case-by-case basis, not a hostage situation.

SOCCER PRACTICE

When my son Grayson was about four years old, he was on a soccer team. But then, wasn't every four-year-old in the United States of America?

He's one of those kids who wakes up in fifth gear every day. Some mornings before the sun is even up, my son is. He never sleeps in! Which means I can't either. He comes padding down the hallway, and my first thought is usually: "Oh my gosh, too early. Why did I ever have sex with your mother?" Of course, I'm always thrilled when he knocks on the bedroom door and says, "Hey guys, wanna play a game? Guys? HEY! GUYS!" His energy is contagious, his spirit is angelic, and he is a better person than I was even at five years old.

On Tuesday afternoons, Grayson had soccer practice at 3 p.m. I would take him to practice a little early so we could have some father and son time, just him and me, male bonding and all of that healthy family stuff.

On one particular day, we'd kicked the soccer ball around for a good half hour before I realized the coaches were late. It was only about 3:15, but this had not happened before with this team. I thought, huh, unusual, but I continued to kick the soccer ball around with my boy. I mean, why complain about extra time with your child?

This continued for about another half an hour before other parents and their kids went home. Eventually, there was only one other dad and his son. I started to get angry. I thought about the level of commitment from the coaches and how it didn't measure up with the kids and the parents they were actually working for. My first thought was: There better be a good excuse for them shining us on like this! I hadn't taken time off on a Tuesday afternoon to wait for a couple of knuckleheads who don't know about responsibility and dedication to duty.

I walked over to Grayson, got down on one knee, looked him in the face, and said, "Hey, little man. I don't think we're gonna be having practice today." He said, "Why not, Dad?"

"Well, son, your coaches didn't show up."

"Gee, Dad . . . I hope they're OK!"

My chin sank to my chest. I couldn't even look into my son's eyes. My brain stopped like a train hitting a mountain. I was embarrassed and hated myself for what I had thought.

For forty-five minutes, I had been considering the situation, the consequences, the conversation I would have with those guys, the message I was going to send, and the commitment they would be giving me moving forward. Me me me me me.

Not once did I think, "Gosh, I hope they're OK."

I bet I had gone through 300 thoughts. Not one was about them. Instead, I had spent the last forty-five minutes thinking about myself.

One big, long, strong, wrong thought. Something like: "I'm being disrespected again!"

First Thought Wrong!

Chapter 1 Wrap-Up

I have always described addiction as energy without grace. It seems to be the simplest distribution of truth without having to wallow in shame or be confused about genetics or nature versus nurture or "why me?" or any of the other arguments around DNA. It is a painfully unhealthy way to exist.

I'm a firm believer that addicts do what addicts do . . . Until they don't.

Users like me either get help or die.

Addicts, alcoholics, codependents (addicted to the addicted), etcetera are born perfectly broken. Chemically challenged, financially irresponsible, linguistically awkward, socially fearful, spiritually delayed, emotionally inconsistent, intermittently honest, and morally flexible. And it's nobody's fault.

They are bright, beautiful, focused, energetic, creative, determined, and committed when it suits them.

They're not stupid; they're selectively intelligent.

They are not untalented; they are selectively directed with their gifts.

Addicts are divinely fractured human beings who have incredible skills but choose to use them only when it seems to abuse them.

For this particular part of humanity, it is perfectly natural for them to practice behavior that is not their fault, but it is their responsibility to adjust once it is discovered to be harmful or even fatal.

That's part of the equation most traumatized people won't look at: What will YOU do with what was done TO you?

I'm one of those people. And I believe I was born that way: perfectly broken. For me, FTW, First Thought Wrong, is a real thing. It is physically present. Your first thought may be inappropriate, inaccurate, cruel, self-centered, judgmental, ungrateful, whiny, belligerent, criminal, punishing, dishonest, avoidant, biased, blaming, or unbalanced. A bunch, a sliver, a fraction, a hint or more of FTW. First Thought Wrong!

Sometimes my second thought is wronGER! Then my third thought is worse, and my fourth thought is worser. I've had one wrong, long, strong thought that lasted for years. FTW is my problem. Alcohol, narcotics, abuse, sugar, caffeine, screen time, sex, or anything else that changes my mood? Those are all symptoms of First Thought Wrong.

My worst day? When FTW wakes up before I do! I've had mornings when I woke up at 6 a.m., and my brain was FTW at 4:30 a.m.!

My best day is when I can manipulate First Thought Wrong into Next Right Thing. What I often refer to as a "manageable level of cuckoo."

Reflection Section:

Identify three examples of First Thought Wrong in your recent or distant past. How did things progress from that very first thought?

How would these things have progressed differently (better) if you had simply planted your feet, taken a few deep breaths, and touched each one of your teeth with your tongue BEFORE you reacted to that first thought?

Quick fix here: the exact OPPOSITE of the very first thought is a good place to start searching for a healthier direction. For example—FTW: "Lash out verbally!" Second thought: Calmly say nothing.

Chapter 2

If You Have to Keep It a Secret, Don't Do It

Every secret I ever kept festered. Secrets warped me and felt like a weight I had to carry. Overburdened and saturated with untruths or lack of freedom is a difficult way to go through life.

THAT DARNED TWENTY DOLLAR BILL

In early 1976, I had a very beautiful girlfriend. She was my first. It seemed pretty serious at the time, and it had become sexual. I was sure I was in love with her.

I was a junior in high school and pursued her as passionately and respectfully as I knew how at the time.

One Friday morning at school, we were hanging out at the quad and decided to cut class, go home to my house, and make love. I knew no one else would be home. My mother was a schoolteacher, my dad worked at a grocery store during the day, and my younger brothers and my sister would be at school.

Jan and I would have the entire place to ourselves. This would be a first for us, considering most of the times we had had sex we were either in her house, in a car, or at a party somewhere. I could not wait. Ah, youth!

Right before lunchtime at school, we got into my car and drove to my house.

While I checked all the rooms and doors and locks and curtains and nooks and crannies, Jan thought it would be a good idea, a romantic notion, to do that movie scene thing where the woman takes off her shoes and then her socks and then her pants and then her top and then her underpants and then her bra and leaves all of these items in succession down the hallway. Like breadcrumbs for the hungry bird I was.

The only problem was we wound up in my mom and dad's bedroom. Actually, this would be the best place because the bed was big and the room was backed into the farthest part of the house. So if anyone came home early, we could hear them before they got to the end of the hall.

We quickly peeled off my clothes and got down to business. From what I can remember, it was epic. It always was with her.

A short time later, we put our clothes back on. Jan remade the bed, opened the window a little bit, and took a walk around the room, making sure everything was back in its original place. Then we locked up the house and went back to school like nothing had happened. Mission accomplished! What a great Friday that was. Right up until dinnertime.

The Lundholm family ate dinner together that night around 7 p.m. Everyone was in a pretty good mood. The meal was huge, the weather was great, and we were all looking forward to the weekend. As we moved toward dessert, my mother had a question for the kids at the table.

"Which one of you kids was in our bedroom this afternoon?" This was not an unusual question, so nobody answered right away or seemed surprised. Nobody except me. I remember holding my breath, waiting for someone else to respond. My mother said, "I know one of you kids was in our room this afternoon. The window was cracked open, and the bed was made differently than I made it. I wanna know who it was right now." No one answered. We all continued eating dessert. Mom didn't push. I figured the issue would pass.

After the dishes were done, we all went our separate ways in the house.

My brothers David and John and I shared a bedroom. I pulled my brother John aside (He was two years younger than me), and I offered him a deal. I would give him a twenty dollar bill if he would tell Mom that he had been chasing our dog Penny around the house and inadvertently messed up Mom and Dad's bed, remade the bed, and then forgot all about it.

John liked money, so I knew he would do it. None of the boys in our family was new at getting into trouble, but John was emotional and had had his share of consequences for acting out. At fifteen years old, he could take a beating or a lecture. I figured he'd get a lecture. He had the least to lose because he was a little sketchy about focus, and it wouldn't be the first time he had done something and forgotten about it until later. And for twenty bucks? That was a lot of money back then. He'd be OK with this.

I was wrong.

After he explained his fictional story about that afternoon, Mom decided on his punishment. John was supposed to go on a group campout the following weekend, and she decided he would stay home instead. He would miss the campout and think about his family infraction.

John, being the emotional cherry bomb he was, immediately pulled the twenty dollar bill out of his pants pocket and said, "Mark gave me this twenty dollar bill for me to make up the story about the dog on the bed and the mess and the window and the . . . He was with his girlfriend! In YOUR ROOM!"

My good Friday was over. Time for the Crucifixion.

Mom came to my room to give me my consequences. I was put on restriction for one year! Unless I had baseball or basketball practice or had to go to work, I was to be home every afternoon by 4 p.m. For a whole year! Jan's mother was notified, and she took a verbal beating. She also lost a few privileges that summer.

My mother kept the twenty.

MATADOR MOTEL

By October 1988, I was a 120-pound methamphetamine, cocaine wino, shake and bake, look and cook, tweak and peek, thump and bump street guy living under a bridge in Oakland, California.

A one-set-of-clothes, foul-mouthed, long-haired, panhandling criminal.

I couldn't get out of my own way, and I could not stop drinking or taking street drugs. Heroin was especially toxic. There was life in the world, but not in me. I was one of the addicted, walking dead. I'd hit bottom more than once, and now the bottom had hit me. Nowhere left to go. No farther to fall.

One morning, very early, I was looking through a dumpster behind Winchell's donut shop. That particular store used to throw out their day-old donuts still in the pink boxes. For a homeless guy, that was like Christmas morning.

As I approached the dumpster, I noticed a guy on the ground leaning back against it, and I was pretty sure he wasn't breathing. It was forty degrees outside, and I couldn't see his breath.

I recognized him as I got closer. His name was Pedro. He was a pretty tough street guy, and I knew he carried a gun.

He wasn't moving, and that was unusual for Pedro.

After making sure he was dead, I went through his pockets. Found a couple of bucks and a handgun. I got out of the alley as quickly as I could . . . with the money and the gun—minus the donuts.

I'd been considering suicide for quite a while now. Wouldn't speak of it. Not to anyone. For years it drifted around my brain like winter. Cold and bitter and always there. It seemed like ending my life was easier than extending my life. Now I had a gun. At the time, I looked at it like a gift: a sign from God that my time had come. I truly believed this at the time.

For many years, I had stacked up my secrets, one on top of another like bricks in a wall. Cheating on a test in school or a woman I cared about or a business partner I had. Making up different stories about myself or exaggerating things that had happened to me to make me look bigger, better, or more interesting. Hiding a ton of emotion in my chest . . . or insanity in my head.

I was afraid most of the time. Afraid someone would find out the truth about me and hate me as much as I did.

I was lying to people I cared about as I went about my daily business of covering up false behavior, insane thinking, or purely self-centered actions.

The occasional, then consistent, then persistent, then absolutely necessary use of alcohol and many, many other street drugs.

Secrets for me had always been like things I threw into a vault, then locked the door, protecting the secrets from discovery and protecting myself from the secrets.

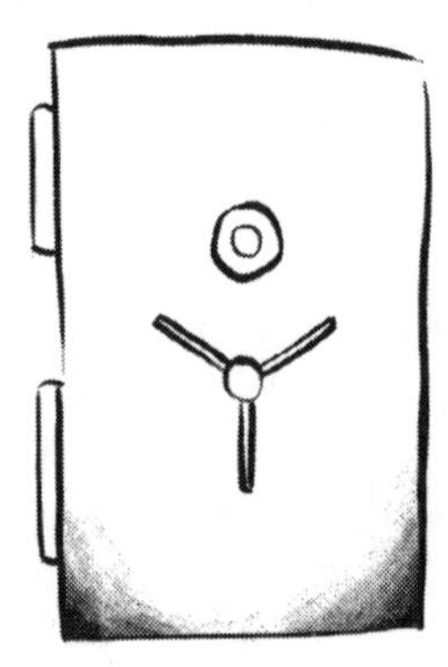

I discovered at some point that when the vault fills up with secrets, it's easy to get locked in the vault too, and there's no dial on the inside.

I was like a top you spun on the table. Put a fast, furious spin on it and watch it dance! The occasional sporting event, falling in love with someone, the healthy and happy partying, the academic victory—these all acted like a temporary twist to keep the top spinning. A new push, a faster spin, a brand-new momentum!

The dishonesty was like an interruption in balance and momentum. The spin started to slow. I'd begun to wobble around and around and eventually couldn't avoid the fall.

Because I knew people in Oakland, I decided to take a bus to Hayward.

I had this strange notion that if I killed myself there, no one I knew would know for a while. Why I believed that at the time, I can no longer remember. Booze will do that to you, I guess.

I just remembered badly wanting to die but not wanting to look bad doing it.

That joke sort of writes itself, yes?

Anyway, I took a bus to Hayward. Eventually, I found myself outside the bathroom window of room 212 at the Matador Motel on Mission Boulevard.

This motel had a six-dollar-per-hour room rate. I didn't have six dollars. I didn't even have one. So I tore the screen off the bathroom window, broke the glass, threw my shirt over the frame, and climbed into the room.

The room smelled just like me: pathetic, foul, and sick. I pulled off my clothes, laid on the bed facing the ceiling, put the gun in my mouth, and pressed it up against the soft, thin skin of the palate. I closed my eyes and pulled the trigger.

Clunk.

The slide on the pistol had jammed.

My immediate reaction was that I was devastated, disappointed. I suck at everything! I pulled the gun out of my mouth and looked at the picture of my daughter on my chest. I had been saving this picture since shortly after her birth. In the photo, she was a newborn—the most innocent thing I had ever seen in my life. Somehow, I had managed to save this picture through all the homeless nights, all the changes of location and clothing. I stared at the photograph and wondered, "How could I do this to her?"

The answer was . . . I couldn't. I decided to get some help instead. In that split second, the moment of clarity was this: I have no idea what I want to do with my life, but I'm sure I no longer want to end it.

Chapter 2 Wrap-Up

A secret means nobody knows. If it's my secret, I know. That makes me nobody. I just got sick and tired of being a nobody in my own story.

I don't know if it's nature or nurture, but for me, secret-keeping feels like instinct. I even keep secrets from myself. Have you ever lied so much that you have legitimately forgotten the truth and believed the lie? A secret is a small dose of truth wrapped in a lie and misdirection, like covering my own tracks so that I can't find my way back.

It took me a few years to learn and then re-learn the difference between secrecy and privacy. I always perceived them as interchangeable. Nope. Secrecy is the prolonged silence surrounding an act of self-centeredness or abuse. Privacy is the protection of self, preservation of internal intimacy, and establishing safety with people and things we cherish. One is hidden under a heap of shame; even when it's First Thought Wrong, it still feels wrong.

The other is love.

One is a curse, and one is a blessing. Love is a blessing.

Like most things in life, it's truly a choice between creating chaos and stress or the K.I.S.S principle: Keep it super simple!

I've discovered that secrets are a whole lot of extra work I've just signed up for. Barnacles on my soul.

Privacy is Mother Nature's natural boundary in a fluid world, a current in the river that flows to a bigger, brighter, better body of water: truth and internal clarity.

My current GPS about honesty is this: If I can't tell my kids about what I'm going to do, I don't do it. That changed my whole life. Respect, integrity, and authenticity come down to your commitment to YOU when no one is watching. So blow yourself a K.I.S.S . . . keep it super simple.

It's been my experience that shame and blame, assaults and lies, sins and secrets are usually hidden somewhere dark. I remember being deathly afraid of the dark when I was a young boy. I still sleep with a nightlight in my bedroom. (These days, it's more so I don't trip over something on my way to the bathroom, but I find it comforting, nonetheless.) I don't know anyone who sees better in the dark. I know that light, when shined upon the unknown or unseen or unsaid, changes everything!

Reflection Section:

What has been the most expensive secret you have kept? What was the cost emotionally, physically, or psychologically?

Do you remember letting go of something secretive and feeling relief, freedom, or growth?

Is there something you are holding on to NOW that should be brought out into the open?

Chapter 3

What You Give Energy to Will Continue

Addiction is energy without grace. You could say the same for the word "failure."

There are no mistakes in the universe. The natural gifts or talents I was given became liabilities and weapons instead of tools. Poor direction. Where I aim myself is where I will find myself.

THE SANTA CRUZ COMEDY SHOW

Sometime in the 1990s, I was doing a series of one-nighters in Idaho, Montana, Nevada, Oregon, and Washington. I was making my way back to California and picked up a horrible case of the flu. I had a 103-degree temperature and I could barely breathe.

I was flying from Oregon to San Jose, California, on a tiny plane early on a Sunday morning. I know I have been sicker in my life, but I honestly could not remember when at that point in the trip. I was sick and tired and sweating and shaking, and I could hardly stand up on my own two feet . . . and I had a 7 p.m. show that night in Santa Cruz. The Crow's Nest. One of the top comedy spots in the Bay Area, but only on Sunday nights. The rest of the week, it was a fantastic beach food joint. Very popular, but especially packed to the rafters on Sunday nights for comedy. I had a sold-out show to perform . . . with the flu. How funny can you be with the flu? Well, I was about to find out.

I had a girlfriend at that time named Gina. She was one of the ones that got away. There have been two or three of those in my life. She was kind and supportive, and loyal above all else. She never minded that I was on the road for weeks at a time doing what I loved to do, calling it work. In seven years, she had never been anything but helpful and patient when it came to supporting me. Thank you, Gina. I still love her for that.

She picked me up at the San Jose airport and immediately recognized something was dreadfully wrong. I could hardly stand up, I was soaking wet with sweat, and I was experiencing almost seizure-like waves of shivering. She wrapped her arms around my neck and realized I was on fire. We took my temperature at 5 p.m. that Sunday evening: 104 degrees. The show was in two hours, and I was sick enough to go to the emergency room. But we didn't go to the emergency room. We took the hour-long drive over the Santa Cruz mountain range to the Crow's Nest for the comedy show. Oh, and one more thing . . . I had gone deaf from the pressure in the plane and the stuffiness in my head. I literally could not hear a single sound. Nothing.

I had been doing comedy for six or seven years professionally by this time. Despite my selective hearing, I had never done a show where I couldn't hear the audience's applause or boos or the hecklers or waitstaff or instructions from the owner or the MC. I also couldn't have a conversation with my girlfriend on the drive over. But I needed the money from that performance, and I was absolutely in a panic about how to do a show where I couldn't hear anything. When a comedian speaks, there's a short period where the audience responds. They will laugh, applaud, wait, or drift. If a comedian talks too quickly, he steps on a laugh. If he waits too long, he appears needy, like he's hoping for laughter. Comedy is all about timing. And timing is all about listening. What in the hell was I going to do???!

Gina wrote me a note and handed it to me when we got to the club.

"Mark. You're going to have to trust me. I've seen your shows so many times, and I know the material so well that I can help you tonight. You can do the show, but you're going to have to trust me. Here's what we'll do: you go through your show and as you finish the punchlines, look at me. I will nod my head when the audience's laughter or applause has started to die down to the point where you can start the next joke. You talk, I'll nod my head, you talk again. We can do this together if you let me guide you."

I thought to myself, "No damn way am I gonna let somebody else be in charge of my performance and put my faith in somebody who's not even a comedian! I'll have to cancel the show!" Right then, the owner walked up to me, took one look, and said, "Jesus H. Jesus, son. You look like a sack of hammered shitcakes! You dying?" I paused, looked at Gina, who nodded her head, and I said, "No, I'm good to go, Boss." And I was. And Gina was. And the crowd was.

The show began with the MC announcing my credits, where I was from, and how many times I'd been on television, yadda, yadda, yadda. I didn't hear a thing. I was too busy off to the side of the stage, worrying about how bad the show was going to be and how guilty I would feel about taking money for a horrible effort on my part. I peeked around the side curtain and saw Gina sitting in the front row. She could not have looked happier. She always had this way of knowing things were going to turn out OK. Her intent was always so pure. How else could it go? It was faith. She nodded at me, and I came walking out right on time.

As I made my opening joke, I could see the people laughing, but I could not hear a single sound. So I followed Gina's direction. I would talk, she would nod, I would talk, she would nod, I would pause, she wouldn't nod, then she would nod, and I would talk.

As the night danced on, she and I got into a perfect rhythm. The performance was solid, the crowd was pleased, the owner paid me, and I thanked Gina. She just did her usual "Oh shucks, I'm humble, that's what partners do" thing. And she handed me a note. "Thank you for trusting me." I nodded my head. And I remember thinking: that's one of the best shows I've ever done in my life. At least, that's what I heard.

It seems that every time I've been invited to spend energy in an unhealthy direction, it's like gravity pulling me down. On the other hand, healthy directions like levity, civility, clarity, purity, and positivity guide me upward and make my path simpler, my vision sharper, and my experience more productive. True, these things do require more effort on my part, but isn't that what life is? You take away what you put in?

Once I began to choose the lighter, cleaner way of living and thinking and moving toward hope, I felt lighter and more focused on the opportunities I've been given, like the power of choice. Today I can rely on choice, not chance. I choose to believe that hope becomes belief and fear becomes faith and that I make a conscious decision to rotate or aim myself toward the greater good. I'm convinced that there's a force of love and light in the universe that provides for me and allows me to thrive. That is, unless I let gravity take over.

In the past, when challenged, I sometimes took an active role and stepped up, but other times I let the weight take me down. Even If I avoided the unhealthy consequences and scraped by the negativity, I considered myself lucky. When something went my way, I would often explain it by saying, "Wow. I sure got lucky there." And then an old friend of mine would say to me, "You still calling it luck?"

CHRISTMAS SURPRISE

In 2012 or 2013, Grayson and I spent Christmas Eve together. His mother and I were divorced, and we had joint custody. It was an extremely painful time for me, but it was challenging for all three of us. Divorce is always hard, even when it's amicable and necessary. It always reminds me of surgery: it has to be done. It's no fun at the time. You've got to have a lot of help during the procedure. And everybody hopes that they are healthier as a result of the process.

One more thing I can pass along here. There are no ex-children in any divorce. Children are not line items on a balance sheet, bargaining chips, or pieces of real estate. They are your kids, on loan to you from the universe. How you care for and educate your children is your gift back to the universe.

My ex-wife Julee and I were and still are very aware of our jobs as parents. That is not to say that it's always been easy to remember the priorities from day to day or from challenge to challenge. It's certainly a learn-as-you-go kind of thing.

This particular Christmas morning, Grayson and I were playing around in my living room, looking at the few simple presents we had exchanged the night before. It was a lovely holiday for us so far. At five years old, Grayson was bright, loving, polite, and responsible; he was a joy to raise and a privilege to live with. There were times when I hated to give him up and take him over to his mother's house. It had nothing to do with the divorce or his mother. I just missed the hell out of him!

Being a present father had a way of centering me. Usually children inherit something from their father, but Grayson bequeathed a dimension of healing to my soul. He embodied safety, connection, and trust—all things absent in my childhood. I'm not the father I had; he's not the child I was . . . It's amazing.

This was one of those times when I wanted to keep him the entire holiday week. But the arrangement his mother and I had made was that I got him Christmas Eve and Julee got him Christmas Day. That day, as we played in the living room, I looked up at the clock on my living room wall and realized it was time to bundle him up and deliver him to his mother. Dammit.

He and I did the job together. We packed a bag of his clothing, necessities, gifts to take to his mother, and the special present he had received the night before: a dump truck.

Back then, Grayson was mesmerized by heavy equipment tractors, trucks, and anything to do with digging or hauling. He was a voracious reader, and even his books were about paving and grading and garbage trucks and earthmoving and heavy loaders. Nice and dirty!

He carried an armload down the stairs from my apartment to my '98 Chevy Silverado pickup truck, me following sadly behind him. Christmas Day was going to be a little lonelier in a few minutes. His mom was only five minutes away from my place.

I did my best to keep my melancholy to myself. As we walked out to the truck, Grayson turned back to look at me and said: "Merry Christmas, Dad. BDE. Best day ever!" For him, it was about the day! For me, it was all about . . . myself.

As we passed through the security gates and out onto the street, I noticed that my truck wasn't sitting quite right. The front left corner was lowered a little bit. The whole damn truck wasn't level now. What the . . .?

I slowly came around the back end of the vehicle, and I couldn't

believe what I was looking at. A knife. A big knife sticking out of my left front tire sidewall. Quicker than the speed of light, I went from sad to homicidal. SNAP . . . Like that! Flooded with First Thought Wrong! I want somebody dead. I want their family dead. I want their neighbors and anyone who even looks like them . . . dead. And oh, by the way, let's not forget that it's Christmas morning. I can't see straight, I can't think straight, and I'm going to do whatever it takes to get even with whoever this was. I was so caught up in my head and the futuristic fantasy of someone's fatality that I didn't hear Grayson speaking to me softly: "Hey Dad, is that a knife?"

I responded through clenched teeth, half-mad at him now for being a little idiot, pointing out the obvious. Thank you, genius. "Yes, son, that is a knife."

Grayson said, "Gee, Dad, that's a nice knife." And it was a nice knife. It had a nice, carved bone handle and a broad, wide blade. This knife might've cost a few bucks.

Evidently, somebody who'd shoved it in the side of the tire hadn't been able to pull it back out or had almost gotten caught in the middle of the act. I had spent enough time as a criminal to know that you don't just abandon an effective weapon, especially when it probably has fingerprints on it.

My first thought was, "I'll use some friendly police resources to identify the culprit from his fingerprints, and then I'm going to hunt him down and kill him."

Once again, out of the misty mayhem in my head, I heard a tiny little voice: "Well, Dad, I have good news and bad news."

"Really?" I replied. "What's the bad news, kid?"

Grayson responded, "Duh, knife in your tire?" He got me there.

I smiled just a little bit. "OK, what's the good news?"

Grayson said gleefully, "Only one of your tires is flat, Dad!" I started giggling, laughed pretty hard, watched him laugh with me, and felt the judge and jury drain out of my brain.

Suddenly I could not take my eyes off that little junior Jesus, that baby Buddha I was raising.

As if he was reading my mind and to cement this exact sentiment, he said: "Dad? Did you ever do stuff like this when you were a criminal?"

Once again, I had to think backward, slowly, thoroughly, past the first few thousand thoughts I'd had since seeing the knife in my tire. Whenever I take the time to think past the first thought, balance shows up. Grace and humility buoy whatever negativity wants to consume me at the time. Honesty, especially when it comes out of the mind and mouth of a child we make, makes all the difference in the world at that moment. Where I AIM myself is where I will find myself.

I still have that knife. The universe gave me a little extra time with my son on Christmas Day.

When my focus returned to real life and the holiday and the blessings I have had, including that little boy—and the ability to tell stories or make humor out of offenses in our lives—I wrote a joke. I still use this joke sometimes. It goes like this:

"The difference between most people and alcoholics is . . . The average person comes out to the car and finds a flat tire and fixes it. An alcoholic comes out to find a flat tire on their car and flattens the other three tires so that the ride is level now."

GOOD, GOD, OR GUIDE?

I remember being told as a little boy that God loved me. The church, my parents, the teachers in Catholic school, and everyone on my street said so! I took that on faith, of course. The evidence I saw to the contrary was overwhelming the older I got. Religion and spirituality and God and kindness and love and mercy might as well have been stories in a Dr. Seuss book. Those notions came from someone's imagination to make kids feel better about the truth. Life was hard. People needed to be harder. Life was mean. People needed to be meaner. The evidence for that was also overwhelming, and I continued to look at that side of the argument for many, many years. I was myopic when it came to fairness and balance and goodness. They weren't real. Reality was selfish and judgmental and cruel, and being nice made you weak, being vulnerable made you a target, and practicing honesty meant you were soft and disrespected. I chose to look at life that way for a long, long time.

After a while, I couldn't help myself. I came to believe that the feelings I had as a human being regarding religion and faith in God had turned 180 degrees from how I had been brought up in the church. The lower I slid down the mountain, the easier it was to keep sliding, stop believing, and start drinking or using drugs. At this point in the book, the reader is well aware of my past history in and around substance abuse. From the time I was five years old, I used sugar, television, attention, performance, academics, alcohol, romance, weed, cocaine, methamphetamine, heroin, arrogance, violence, and too many more to count as substitutes for higher education, faith in a God of my understanding, connections to truth and family, and healthy relationships.

When I was about two years sober, I was living down in the South Bay area of northern California. I was a twelve-step-meeting guy, working on recovery issues and sobriety stuff as well as I could possibly manage without believing in God. I didn't call myself an atheist or an agnostic or a free thinker. Simply put, I really didn't believe in anything besides what I could see with my own eyes.

I did the best I could to follow directions from people who seemed to know what they were doing or appeared to have some kind of plan to stay out of trouble and change their own lives. Freeman G. was one of those people. He was my sponsor at the time, and I looked up to him because he seemed sure of himself, was incredibly popular, and spoke in large groups like he was a cross between Jesus Christ, Martin Luther King, and Elvis Presley. He was a true leader and orator.

One day, in a terribly confused state, I approached him and said simply: "Freeman, I just don't get the spiritual side of all this recovery and sobriety stuff!"

He said, "Oh man, that's too bad. Because it's ALL spiritual!" He went on to say that "spiritual" was just a way of saying truthful and helpful. No big deal, kiddo! It was like listening to a GOOD parent, or a KIND teacher, or a GENTLE police officer. I thought to myself, "I used to know some of those people, and they were all women." Maybe I had a chance to really believe in something here. Show me something I could actually see with my own eyes.

My God has been a Goddess ever since.

GOD. Stands for Great Opportunity Daily, and GOD is the first syllable of the word "goddess." This is what I believe as I traverse the daily path from zero to hero. From now to wow! From drinking and sinking to living and giving. From using and losing to praying and staying.

Every day, I find a way to let the great universal mother care for me as a child of God. And here's the best part: If I stay out of her way but in her light, I've got a really good chance of doing the right thing in the right way for the right reason.

I've discovered that where I point my prayers is where I'll discover my faith. After many years, I've come to a point where I don't just believe because things started to get better. Things got better because I started to believe.

Chapter 3 Wrap-Up

Trust is a fantastic compass point. Whether it's a girlfriend who helped me when I had given all of my energy to poor self-care or a young boy who redirected me from rage to gratitude.

Bonus shortcut here: Whatever you thought about most yesterday was your higher power for yesterday. Where did you aim yourself during the day, and where did you find yourself when the day was done?

Did any of the following DRIVE you yesterday: hate, hurt, lust, money, fear, resentment, doubt, panic, punishment, ego? I'm not judgin', I'm just sayin'.

What or who was driving yesterday? What a relief it was to discover the freedom of choice I had when it came to faith. God, good, goddess, grace, guide, GPS, beauty, nature, energy, love, power, process, purpose, passion. Pick one! They all work as a compass for truth, trust, growth, and health.

Try this just once: Fill in the blank with any of the words I've suggested above.

PRAYER

"Thank you _____ for another day clean and sober. Help me to stay clean and sober today. Help me to be honest and humble. Let me be willing to do your will, not mine. Please watch over everyone I love and everyone I don't. I'd like to say a special prayer for all of those with whom I have resentment. I wish for them all the things I want for myself: a working relationship with a higher power, inner peace and serenity, the love of family and friends, and freedom from financial insecurity."

Reflection Section:

What truth or criticism did you hear recently that you didn't like hearing or didn't want to hear but helped you in spite of those feelings?

What happens when you practice slowing down in the middle of having intense feelings and ask yourself, "Am I taking this personally or looking at this truthfully?"

Can you name a specific event or interaction in your life where you chose not to give energy to anger, argument, negativity, or First Thought Wrong?

Chapter 4

You Are What You Answer To

The toughest lessons are always the most rewarding and valuable. Criticism or reviews or the judgment of others always gives me a choice: I can take it personally or look at it truthfully. Only one of these choices is healthy. The other is always the deadest of ends.

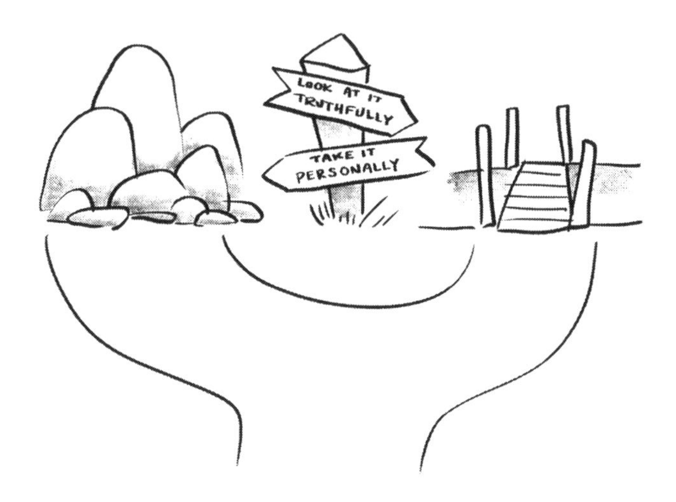

MAGIC MR. EARL

Back in the early 1960s, I was living in Oakland, California. I attended pre-K, kindergarten, and first grade in a predominantly black neighborhood where my super white Caucasian Nordic family was a minority, but nobody in town cared what color anybody was.

It was a really sweet time in the 'hood. The funny thing was: Everyone knew everyone. We knew all of our neighbors' names and schedules; we watched the neighbors' kids when the parents worked a double; we barbecued together after Sunday service; we brought food to each other when folks on the street were sick or out of work. It was truly a neighborhood.

But kids will also be kids. As a young boy, a lot of the kids in the neighborhood called me N----r Lips. As a child, I had lips covering a third of my face. At least that's how it felt to me and evidently looked to some other people.

I didn't know whether to be embarrassed or not. I just knew that that word was supposed to hurt people's feelings. It devastated me.

Every day as I'd walk to or from school, that name was tossed at me like some kind of acid. Not from kids who knew me well but from kids who were too ignorant to understand that we're all in this together.

Oakland was a strong city back in the sixties. Industrial, political, historical, important.

Every family I knew that lived on our street was proud to be exactly where we were at the time. Pride is a lot like prejudice: It doesn't care about finance, romance, circumstance, education, politics, address, ZIP code, or where you want to point your prayers. Pride crosses all borders and bigotry.

One particular dreary afternoon, I wandered home from kindergarten by myself, as usual, trying not to hear the ugly names thrown my way. Our next-door neighbor Mr. Earl—at times, the dad I wish I had back then—was tending to his front lawn. His yard was always immaculate: perfectly green, manicured grass surrounded by a tall cyclone fence, some low hedges, and patrolled by a huge German Shepherd. As I walked along the sidewalk past his yard, Mr. Earl noticed I was crying.

He asked, "Hey popcorn, why you crying?" You see, Mr. Earl had names for the kids in my family based on the shade of white we were. I was Popcorn. My sister was Paper, and my brother was Albino. My youngest brother was Snowman. It's just the way it was back then, and none of us took it personally because we knew he liked and respected us. Mr. Earl was my friend. These were special nicknames for special kids who lived next door to a special man. Nothing personal.

I said, sobbing, "Mr. Earl, every time I walk home from school, somebody calls me 'N----r Lips.' I know they want to hurt me, and it works."

"N-----r Lips, huh? Well . . . ARE you?"

I sniffled. "Mr. Earl, I don't know."

"Hey boy, I'll tell you something: You are what you answer TO! Don't forget that. If you don't like a name, don't answer to it."

"OK, Mr. Earl . . . Thank you, Mr. Earl."

"Now hurry on past, boy. You know my dog don't like white folk."

That was a fact!

There was power in that sentence: You are what you answer to. The power in that statement stayed with me for the rest of my life. I gave up power to people every time I let their words define who I was. I gave myself power every time I knew who I was, no matter what someone else called me.

The high-wire balancing act was trying not to become one of the people who called other folks names. The shortcut for me here was that a lot of times, the name-calling came FROM me, was received BY me, and continued to be something I answered to: loser, criminal, failure, worthless, nothing, not as good as, less than. All of these names were labels I gave myself throughout my life. Until I didn't.

THE BETTY FORD CENTER EVENING

In 1995, I met Duncan and Kathy James. They were a phenomenal recovery couple who were affiliated with the Betty Ford Center.

I had just finished a ninety-minute show at the Luther Burbank Auditorium in Santa Rosa, California. Duncan and Kathy were fans from Ukiah who came backstage to talk to me about an appearance they wanted me to make at the annual Betty Ford Center alumni reunion.

I had heard of Betty Ford and the Center but had never been there and certainly had not been a patient of that prestigious landmark. I had done my detox and first few weeks of sobriety at a locked-down mental institution in Oakland called Gladman. The Betty Ford Center was glamorous. Gladman hospital had been a revelation. Both places did treatment. But one of them was a lot more upscale and expensive than the other. At this point in my life, I was incredibly used to the idea of being the "other."

Sitting backstage, they explained that there was a big-name headliner for the Betty Ford Center show and that they wanted me to do a twenty-minute comedy set to open the event. I asked Duncan: "It's an alumni reunion, right? I'm not an alum of Betty Ford." He responded, "That's true. You'll be the very first performer who never actually attended the center. Kind of cool, huh?"

I said, "Yeah, cool is one way to say it." I thought to myself, "This might be cool, it might be a big deal, but either way I'm gonna learn something and see something I'll remember." I had no idea how prophetic that statement was.

I wrote out a special fifteen-minute long setlist, planning for five minutes of laughter from the audience. When you're timing a comedy set, you have to allow for laughter. Otherwise, you're going to go long. When it comes to television, radio, or big shows in a casino ballroom, going long is a death sentence. Time is money. I didn't think the Betty Ford Center, with all its affluence and celebrity, would be much different. I was right.

The night of the event started out funny. I had two sets of clothing that evening. I had a black suit and black tie with a white shirt and shiny black dress shoes. I also had a dazzlingly gaudy vest with a tight black t-shirt, black slacks, and black tennis shoes.

I was in my pre-show nice black suit leaning against the back wall of the ballroom of a swank, stunningly gorgeous Palm Springs hotel, La Esmerelda. There were about 1500 people in the audience. Betty Ford could draw a crowd!

As I was standing against the back wall, I noticed Secret Service guys strategically placed around the ballroom, keeping an eye on the former president of the United States, Gerald Ford, and the former first lady, Betty.

I hadn't considered this as I looked around the room and saw people dressed up in their gowns, tuxedos, jewelry, and 300-dollar hairdos. I had never worked for a crowd this wealthy, famous, or important. I found myself mesmerized by the opulence. Just then, an audience member with a tiny plate of hors d'oeuvres in one hand tapped me on the shoulder. He looked at me, my suit, and the Secret Service standing against other walls in the ballroom. He said in a soft, sly voice, "Hey man, how long have you been with the service?"

I tilted my head just a fraction of an inch in the opposite direction from the man, and I said in my lowest baritone voice, "It's a secret."

He popped his head back and said, "Oh, of course. Excuse me, I'm sorry." Then he scooted off in another direction. I smiled a little and thought, "I'm going to be really good tonight."

Then I met John Boop. John was the marketing director of the Betty Ford Center and a long-time legendary iconic figure in Palm Springs: a very important man that evening. He wanted to remind me of that. He said, "I'm John Boop. I've never heard of you, and I don't know how you got this job tonight, but here's how it's gonna go. You will not embarrass the Betty Ford Center. You will not address, speak to, or even look at the President or Mrs. Ford. You will not make us look bad this evening. Do you understand? You will not cause a scene or create any controversy or other unpleasant situation. I didn't get a chance to vet you or OK your material. But you can be darn sure that I'll have my eye on you tonight, understand?"

Very, very slowly, I took a step toward him, straightened my tie, looked away for a second, then said, "Hey, John. You've got to work on your attaboy." And I walked away to change my clothes for the show.

After the dope deal gone bad, thug-life-in-jail exchange between Mr. Boop and myself, I was just a little bit angry and not in the right mood to do a good set. I had written great material for that night, tailored specifically to the Betty Ford Center, the recovery experience, and a very Republican, politically correct crowd. I had brought all the right stuff, and now I felt stained by that conversation.

Then I remembered Mr. Earl back in the Oakland neighborhood I grew up in: "You are what you answer to, boy." Time to go to work.

I put on my hideous multicolored vest, spiked my hair, and waited on the side of the stage for my introduction. "Ladies and gentlemen, please welcome the very funny Mark Lundholm."

I began with a respectful thank you and a couple of lighthearted jokes about dysfunctional families, the huge ego that an alcoholic has to go along with his or her low self-esteem, and the fact that I love a recovery audience. "Welcome to the Betty Ford Center, where ACA stands for Adult Child of an Actor. Alcoholics, my favorite crowd. In the parking lot this evening, I did two things. Because I love you, I said a little prayer. Because I know you, I locked my car." The set continued steadily, and I was connecting with a discerning, educated audience.

Then I took a risk. I looked at table number one, the Ford table. I said, "Mrs. Ford, it is my extreme honor to work for arguably the most powerful person in the free world . . . and your husband." Huge laugh. Then I said, "But I have a question. With all the good you've done here, with all the influence you have here tonight, with all the humility and grace that you've shown this country about alcoholism, if you did relapse, where would you go for treatment? I mean, it's pretty hard to be humble when your name is on everything. In every building every day, and everybody who works here works for you!" Turning to the audience, I said, "Mrs. Ford, you need to go to group now. Mrs. Ford? You need to go to group now! Mrs. Ford, will you be going to group today? No? OK, that's fine. Anything we can get you, my dear? Did I mention how much I LOVE working here at the BETTY FORD Center?"

By then, Gerald and Betty Ford were laughing so hard I couldn't lose. The audience tapped the tables, an act tantamount to an applause break.

And then I had a thought. I looked over at the table where I saw John Boop. He met my eyes and gave me a huge smile and two thumbs up. "Attaboy," I thought.

At the end of the evening, John Boop approached me. He said, "Never seen a comedian do a better job here. Honestly. Would you like to meet the President and Mrs. Ford? They each have a receiving line. It happens every reunion."

Of course, I agreed and we wandered over to Mrs. Ford's line. There had to be 150 people waiting to meet her, thank her, or just look at her. Boop walked me to the front of the line, excused the both of us, and said to Mrs. Ford, "I know you wanted to meet this young man. This is Mark Lundholm." Right away, she noticed the vest (it was hard to miss), shook my hand, gave me a warm hug, and said, "Thank you for speaking to my husband and I. A lot of performers are afraid to do that, I guess. Your comedy was precious. Would you care to take a photograph with my husband and myself?" I joked, "Do you think we need him?" She laughed, grabbed my arm, turned me around, and we took a picture together. Just the two of us. I still have it.

John Boop and I became friends. He's treated me like a headliner ever since '95. Since that night, I've worked for the Betty Ford Center at least five or six times. Fundraisers, client workshops, and two more alumni reunions. Mrs. Ford, the President, John Boop, Joan Clark, and especially Duncan and Kathy James have been supportive, professional, and graceful for many, many years now. Duncan and Kathy are godparents to my boy Grayson.

Chapter 4 Wrap-Up

Bonus shortcut: When it comes to events or labels or words themselves, you have two choices. You can take things personally or look at them truthfully. One of those is a waste of time and energy, and one is a learning experience or an opportunity to look at yourself, a teaching moment. I will give you an example.

Very recently, in a process group I was facilitating at a treatment center, I asked the group of inpatients, as I always do: "What word do you not like thrown at you?" I usually get the same ones: the obvious expletives and then words like criminal, failure, and loser.

I always choose the word loser first and say: "Well, are you? Because that's not what I see from where I'm standing. But I don't know you as well as you know you. If it were me and somebody called me a loser, I'd say 'bullseye, buddy, a lot of my life. Still am today.' You see, I've lost that self-centered feeling of 'everything is mine at your expense.' I've lost that Monday morning sense of dread where I don't know what I did during the weekend, but I'm sure I owe someone an apology. I've lost whatever chemical quicksand I used to fall into when alcohol, cocaine, sex, rage, ego, or boredom pulled me into the abyss. In fact, you give me a t-shirt that says 'loser' right on the front of it, I'll wear it all day. On the plane. On stage. At the mall. At the gym. To bed. Because you see, I know what losing really means. Someday I hope all losers will too.

"If I called you a radiator or a pinecone or a cereal bowl, how upset would you be? Hopefully it wouldn't hurt your feelings or create unrealistic expectations or horrible resentment.

"Names, words, labels, and lies are all invitations to ramp up or down emotionally. Emotions can be contagious, depending upon the severity. But feelings are never facts. They can be real. Valid. Justified. False. True. Temporary. They are lots of things. But feelings just aren't facts.

"How often have I reacted or not reacted or taken immediate action based on how I felt in that moment instead of what the facts were at the time? I'll try to 'do it until I'm through it.' I finally discovered that after each feeling, there's another one. If I can survive one, I'll arrive at the next one. Fear becomes faith and respect. Anger becomes a passion to change something. Sadness becomes empathetic and connected. Glad becomes grateful, satisfied, safe, and sure.

"There are no BAD feelings. There are only negative consequences or powerful lessons in truth when I react or remain inert. And the behavior I can no longer afford is . . . Don't feel. Put it somewhere and forget all about it. I spent years putting feelings into an invisible trashcan and slamming the lid down. Eventually, all the trash is still in there. It's overflowing, and I can't find a big enough lid to keep it all in.

"Every time I've been unfairly challenged, personally discounted, or harshly criticized in my life, I've had a part in it. I didn't know that when I was younger, and I could never have figured it out on my own. As a child, I was taught 'sticks and stones may break my bones, but words will never hurt me.' I wish that were true. What I wasn't told was, 'In order to avoid the long-term injury or the severe pain from what is being said to you, you have to look at the truth in those words.'

"If there is truth, it's a definite message. If there isn't any truth in what is being said, those words have the same effect as shooting a BB gun at a freight train. Nice try. Sometimes, the truth is like a scalpel; it has to cut deep to do its work. But when handled properly and used by someone who is trained and caring, it is an amazing tool for healing. So, the question I ask myself now is always: Do I take it personally and become a victim, or do I look at it truthfully and start the recovery process of getting better?"

Reflection Section

Can you think of a time when you reacted to name-calling, a slur, or an accusation emotionally? What did it cost you? Was it the word that hurt, or was it an old memory or painful event?

Do you think if you had slowed down your breathing, your thought process, and your reaction time, you could have taken that opportunity to ask yourself, "Is there any truth in what I just heard?"

Challenge is always an opportunity to change for the better. How can you use the shortcut in this chapter as a tool for personal growth?

Chapter 5

Freedom Starts with Forgiveness

Hate only hurts the person who holds on to it. The people and behaviors that I won't forgive, I most certainly will become. To forgive doesn't mean to condone or excuse or forget the attack or injury. It means, "I'm tired of holding on to the resentment."

KINTSUGI

This is a thousand-year-old Japanese process used when something of value has been broken—a vase, statue, ceramic, or porcelain item—to put it back together using a lacquer containing a precious metal like gold, platinum, or silver. The lacquer fills and highlights the cracks or breaks in the repaired, revitalized object. The breakage is not hidden or disguised; it is magnified and presented as beautiful and necessary and a vital piece of the art. Does that sound like anything—or anyone—you know?

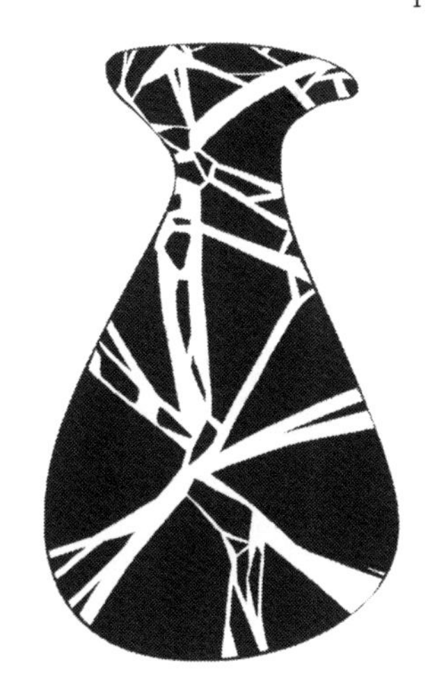

I have long believed that some human beings are born "perfectly broken." By divine design, we are psychologically impaired, socially awkward, linguistically challenged, financially irresponsible, selectively gifted, educationally twisted, visually warped, chemically addicted, spiritually retarded, or morally flexible.

NONE of these characteristics is a handicap or flaw; they are merely hurdles on the path toward health, hope, success, and grace . . . unless they are kept hidden and secret or are a source of shame.

The universe has never created any garbage. Only human beings do that. And the perfectly broken people do it sooner, longer, and more often than most people. That's really the only thing that separates human beings on this planet. What do you do with damage when you find it? Identify it and get to a solution? Or use it as an excuse to fail or continue being different until you die from it?

I believe that when I find a flaw in myself, I have a responsibility to identify its depth, ask for help, seek treatment, and do the repair for it, then show others how I repaired it.

The highlighting of a loss or mistake or injury is a beautiful part of the human experience. It acts as a beacon to others who are "broken" in the same places. We do these things FOR ourselves WITH one another. And the lacquer that puts us back together is truth. Truth is our precious metal. Question: who do you treat better, someone you resent or blame, or someone you have forgiven?

We don't all break in exactly the same places. If we are broken together at the same time, it is often difficult to locate our own pieces among the breakage of others. What we do for ourselves takes time. If we are willing to take the time to mend ourselves using the truth as adhesive, binding lacquer, only then can we pass the process and healing along to the next generation of perfectly broken human beings.

And through experience, hope, and strength, we may be able to quicken that process for those we assist. This is where the term "shortcuts" comes from. Those of us who have healed and done some work by repairing our own damage can give the next group a shortcut or two. Or more. Forgiveness is a shortcut.

WOMB CONVERSATIONS

My ex-wife Julee and I were married in 2005. We were very much in love and hopeful of our life together. She became pregnant in 2006. In March of 2007, Grayson Cole Lundholm was born. It was one of the single greatest days of my life—and the subject of this particular story.

From the very first day of Julee's pregnancy, I made it a point to talk to the child in her womb. Male or female, indoor plumbing or outdoor plumbing, I didn't care. I just wanted to talk to that brand new human being who was the product of two phenomenal people with phenomenal stories, incredible talents, and spectacular gifts. What a special little person it was that was destined to pop out of this lady, made by this man, cooked by this mother, protected by this father, honored and cherished by this mother and father.

I would have short or sometimes incredibly long conversations with the little person in my beautiful wife's belly.

At first, Julee thought it was cute and unique. But eventually it got annoying to her. I couldn't care less what anyone else thought. I was speaking to a person I already loved and respected. A new human being to the planet, a perfect addition to the family, and a fresh start for two people who had prayed for that for a long time.

We really could've named our son Hope. But I love the name Grayson for two reasons. One, gray is my favorite color. It's the color of wisdom; people get gray as they age and survive and struggle. Someone that has arrived at the gray stage deserves to be listened to. And two, gray is the color of no judgment. Life is one huge gray area where we decide and learn and share and communicate and find balance, often without ever having to pick a side and still being able to agree to disagree without being disagreeable or adversarial. Gray is not compromise; it is connection. It is the middle that binds the sides. My son had a chance to be all of that and more: a healer.

Sometimes my chats with him would be fairly serious. Sometimes they would be lighthearted and hilarious. I let the day and the mood dictate the message or direction of the talk. Since I was pretty sure that the conversation would be one-sided every time, I tried to be creative as well.

"Hey little one, this is your dad. At least, we are pretty sure I'm your dad." That's the first joke I ever told my kid. At least, we are pretty sure it was a joke.

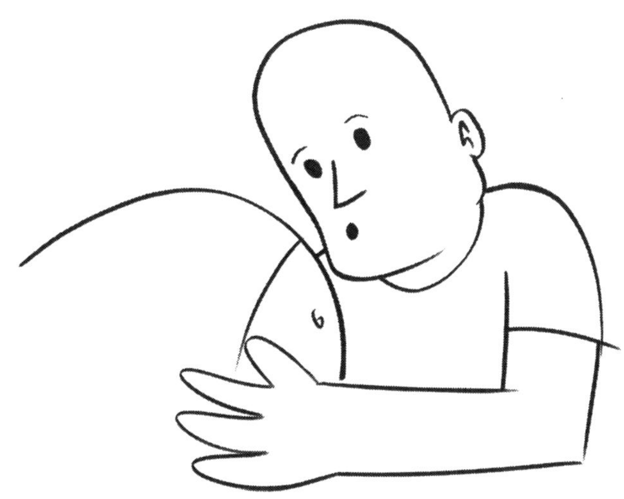

But no matter what the particular topic of conversation was between my new kid and me, the belly was the microphone and the womb was the amplifier. I got to softly whisper into the sanctuary while the little angel rested, slept, or moved about.

We talked about many things: life, love, school, sports, family, weather, clothing, holidays, the future. But no matter where the conversation meandered to, and no matter how long the talk lasted, I always made sure to deliver the same message when we were finished: "Hey, little person. You're in the perfect place at the perfect time, but you never have to be perfect. Be yourself. That will always be good enough. In fact, all you have to do today is soak up the love, get your nourishment, take your sleep, and grow, grow, grow. Everything else will take care of itself. That's all you have to do until you come out. When you DO come out, you have only one job: Honor your mother until your last day on earth. Honor. Your. Mother. If you DON'T honor your mother, I'll make sure it IS your last day on earth. Kidding . . . As far as you know."

The private and semi-private conversations between my son and me were in the hundreds. Of course, I don't remember the text of every single one of them, but I do remember a few that were quite significant: the night his mom was sick and her two men had to be strong for her. The day I was delayed at the airport and missed her birthday so I had her put the cell phone to her belly so that I could tell my son what we bought her as a present. And that Christmas morning when Julee was very large for her size and I mentioned, "Grayson, buddy, you need to take it a little easier on Mom for the next couple of months." The New Year's Day conversation where I mentioned to him, "Hey man, this is your year, the year of Grayson."

At 10 p.m. on a day in late March 2007, we rushed Julee to the hospital because her water had broken. It was time. This is the point where there is no turning back. All the birthing classes and breathing exercises and yoga and groaning and nutrition and the book learning and the doctor talking and meditation and praying would either help or they wouldn't. The kid is coming. The kid is coming now!

As we were assigned a hospital room, one by one, a nurse or physician or intern would come in and check on Julee to make sure she was getting the care she needed, the attention she deserved, and hopefully some rest. She was definitely in labor, but it turns out Grayson was in no hurry to leave the safest place in the history of ever to finally meet the rest of the world.

We didn't know at the time that Julee would be in labor for thirty-two hours straight. Every hour seemed like an eternity that night, the next day, and again, going into dinner time the next night. Mark still waiting, Julee still pregnant, the doctors and nurses still visiting, and Grayson still deciding. Like it or not, he'd be out when he was ready. It turns out that that was right around 2 a.m., thirty-six hours later.

For hours upon hours, my wife and I had laughed and cried and been angry and forgiving and judgmental and crazy and patient. It had been like going to Disneyland and riding every single ride in that park without stopping in between. All the emotions and words and ideas and wishes and dreams had been represented on the last day.

At one point, I had been tested severely. A brand-new physician, one we had never seen before, popped into the room to announce his presence and let us know that he would be beginning his shift. His introduction went something like this: "Hey, I'm Dr. So-and-so, and I will be the attending physician for the next eight hours. And just so you know, I don't mess around. I say what goes and when it happens. I know you want to do this all-natural and stuff, but I'll decide what's safe and when it's time to do this thing. Your doctor told me what you want to happen and that you're willing to let nature take its course, no drugs, blah blah blah. I'll decide. Just so you know who's running things here."

First Thought Wrong: "I'm gonna follow him out of this room, catch him alone, and throw him a beating. I won't let one word come out of his mouth without punching it back through his teeth and out the base of his skull."

I was exhausted and threatened and livid at the time. I looked at Julee, and she just shook her head from side to side. "No, honey. I need you here."

It took every ounce of willpower and recovery skills and concentration on the love of my wife and child to slow me down. Slow me down so I wouldn't hurt that doctor and ultimately myself and my family.

I had twenty or thirty thoughts before I responded to Julee. "Thank you, honey. It's OK, I'm not going anywhere."

I sat next to the bed and watched her sleep. My heart was racing, and my head was spinning. Eventually I laid my head back and tried to get comfortable in the chair. We were both in this for the long haul, and it had already been a long haul. As I nodded off, I thought about the forgiveness I needed to send that little Hitler doctor's way. I said a little prayer, and a short time later, I was out.

I woke up because I heard someone struggling. Disturbing noises and motion.

It was Julee.

The labor pains had begun to intensify, and the contractions were coming closer together. As tough as this lady was, I could tell that she was in a world of hurt. I felt helpless and insignificant, watching her carry this weight alone. No woman can be overestimated or praised enough during the birth of any child. What a miraculous live event, and it takes place hundreds of times a day. I'm convinced it's the single greatest miracle on the planet. And every single living creature is proof of that miracle.

I grabbed her hand—she squeezed harder than she'd ever squeezed my hand before—just as a doctor, our little female Asian doctor, all five-foot-nothing of her, burst through the door. "Everybody ready? Let's do this!" I followed directions and got the hell out of the way.

That doctor was a hurricane inside a tornado during an earthquake. She worked and maneuvered and orchestrated and directed like nothing or no one I had ever seen before. But Grayson still wasn't coming out. I could see the frustration in Julee's eyes, and I could hear it in her breathing. I could tell that even the doctor was losing patience with the situation as she said, "OK, it's come down to this. I'm going to use a vacuum. We're going to attach the suction to the top of your boy's head, and I'm going to gently draw him out whether he likes it or not. But, Mama, you have to push! I cannot do this without your help! Either you push this kid out this time, or I'll have to cut you open. Now, do you want to get cut? It's all up to you, Mama!"

For the second time in twenty-four hours, I wanted to punch a doctor right in the mouth. Then I digested the words she had just used. She was exactly right. This is a team effort between mother and doctor. I was amazed how quickly I realized that Grayson's entrance into this life existed because of these two WOMEN. And THEY didn't need me or my misdirected anger and fatigue . . . at all. I really needed to forgive myself and everybody in this situation if I was going to be here for the best part of it. Forgiveness was the difference between being present for one of the single greatest days of my life and hearing about the event while sitting in jail for assault. Forgiveness allowed me to be a part of everything instead of just . . . apart.

The doctor put the suction cup on the top of the baby's skull and gently started to pull while Julee furiously started to push. All of a sudden, I heard the doctor exclaim: "Here he comes. Here he comes. Slowly and . . . Yes . . . Yes . . . There we are!"

And there he was. Bright red, ungodly covered in goop, elongated skull so that he looked like Dan Aykroyd on Saturday Night Live's Coneheads. Oh yeah, and he was screaming his balls off!

Grayson was born at exactly 2 a.m. Two o'clock in the morning is closing time for bars in the state of California. I still giggle at that fact.

I remember myself making some kind of noise out loud. Something came out of me, like a cross between a caveman grunt, a little girl cry, and a lion's roar. The doctor pulled him all the way out, someone cut the cord, and my son was held up high by two capable, educated, loving hands: his doctor's. She was telling him to "Shush shush shush" and "It's OK, baby, it's OK, baby," but he was having none of it.

I guess being pulled out of a nice warm environment and having a big pointy-headed skull would make me grumpy too. But he screamed and screamed and kicked and punched, and as the doctor held him out in front of her, I stepped up to within a couple of feet of my new son, and I said quietly, "Hey little man, I knew you could do it. I just knew you could do it. Good job, buddy."

He stopped screaming. He stopped kicking and punching. He stopped everything and turned his head in my direction. He was still and alert, and his breathing slowed. He looked directly at me, and I said again, "Hey, little man." And the doctor said, "He knows you. He knows your voice. He already knows who his daddy is." I told the doctor that I had been talking to him for a long time now. Ever since the day we met, I had been talking to my son. Just then—because she was never one to be ignored—Julee added,

"Yep, that's his daddy. Talk talk talk talk talk talk talk talk talk talk talk talk talk."

Forgiving that little male dictator of a doctor allowed me the freedom to hear those words from my wife, be present for the first sights and sounds of my son, and best of all, stay out of jail on Grayson's birthday.

PERPETRATOR CYCLE

One of the side effects of being a humorist is that I am privileged to work with thousands of people every year who are afflicted with or challenged by addiction. I'm not a clinician, and I have no letters after my name, but it's been my experience that almost 100 percent of these individuals, and I am guesstimating here, have experienced a large amount of physical, sexual, or emotional trauma. I know I have. All of the above. Family of origin. A priest in my church. Romance, circumstance, and young adult trauma. I've worked with hundreds of thousands of people in residential treatment centers, correctional facilities, sober living communities, and hospitals. More than thirty years of meeting addicts, alcoholics, and trauma survivors have taught me one fundamental theme: Every single one of them is connected to the others by at least the single thread of punishment. Trauma comes in many forms, not the least of which are self-loathing and verbal abuse. Substance abusers punish. Society, family, friends, and especially themselves.

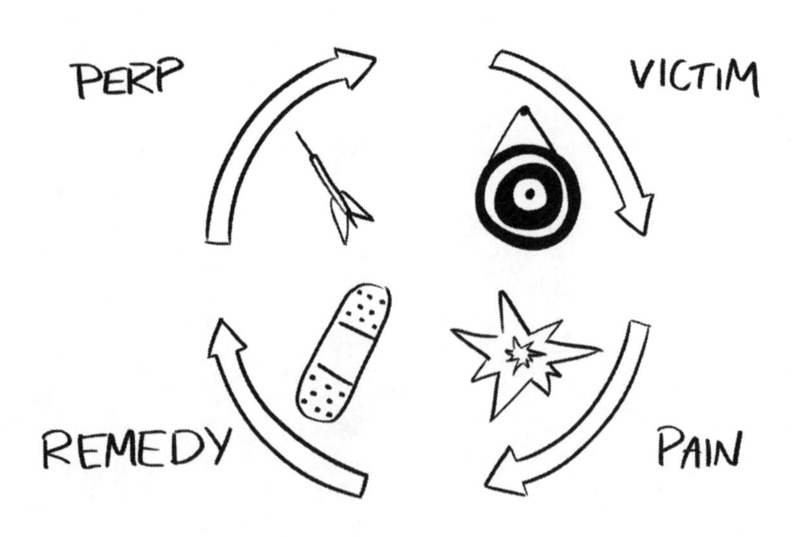

It helps to see what this looks like in picture form, so I've included a diagram here in the story. In process group we call it the "Perp Cycle." Of course, "Perp" is short for "perpetrator." The younger readers probably learned that word from the TV show CSI or Cops. Some of us older folks learned "perp" from Adam 12, Perry Mason, or LA Law. The show Law and Order was for the generations in between. The point here is that a perpetrator is the one who done it. The victim is the one it got done to. When it comes to addiction and substance abuse, there is no such thing as a victimless crime. Pain is inflicted on the victim by the perpetrator and thus begins the cycle. And here is the saddest part of the tale: When the victim chooses a remedy to alleviate or lessen the pain—alcohol, Molly, opioids, methamphetamine, codependency, sex, overtime at work, food, gambling, electronic distractions, relationships—the remedy BECOMES the next perpetrator. And the cycle goes on, with the addict stuck in the middle as the revolutions of the cycle run over everything and everyone in the addict's path, like a fiery ball of lava traveling 100 miles an hour downhill with no end in sight. Ultimately, the person with a substance abuse problem ends up being the primary perpetrator and the primary victim suffering the longest and most severe amount of pain while trying to provide his or her own remedy for the pain they are causing, mostly to themselves. Crazy. This is truly part of the insanity that physicians, drug counselors, and therapists come up against on the front lines of the addiction battle. Addiction is a mental illness. What's my evidence? Thirty years of working with criminals and perpetrators and their victims. What's my response? Forgiveness. Forgive the perpetrator, and perhaps the victim will find true relief and an effective remedy for the pain. Please don't confuse "forgive" for "condone" or "excuse" or even "forget"!

FORGIVE, in this sense, means to stop carrying the weight of the action or memory or injustice. At some point, it's simply too heavy. How long do you choose to carry the weight of somebody else's ignorance or lack of humanity? I'm not judgin', I'm just sayin'. Who do you treat better and respect and care for more? Someone you resent and continue to punish, or a person you have truly forgiven? That person may be you.

Chapter 5 Wrap-Up

In my own history, long ago and even recently, this was one of the toughest shortcuts to wrap my head around. I couldn't fathom the power of forgiveness because I was so consistently focused on finding fault, placing blame, and assigning punishment. Good God, I'm exhausted right now just thinking about all the work it took to be judge, jury, executioner, and court reporter.

When I lighten up, the jokes about this chase actually write themselves. For me, it goes way past "Let he who is without sin cast the first stone." I can't count the times I've denigrated, belittled, fractured, or abused myself, and then aimed all that rage and "blame thrower" heated energy at someone—or everyone—else. Or pointed it chemically at myself.

Forgiveness. Freedom. Forever.

On a case-by-case basis, one day at a time, one injury at a time, one perpetrator at a time. Letting it go is better than hanging on to it.

Reflection Section:

Can you think of a specific example when you forgave someone for injuring you? Was there freedom or relief as a result? What help or benefit would forgiveness provide you?

What or whom could you forgive right now? Are you on the list of people you need to forgive?

How much energy did you spend this week "punishing" someone?

Chapter 6

The Truth You Tell is Equal to the Help You Will Receive

I spent far too many years not listening to other people. I finally reached a point where the amount of truth I knew, the level of truth I could tell, brought me all the way to the bottom. I learned very late in life the two most important sentences in the English language: "I don't know. Will you help me?"

MISSISSIPPI FARMER

Sometime in the early 1990s, I was blessed with an invitation to do a show in a Mississippi State penitentiary. Correctional facilities are some of my favorite places to work and probably will always be a passion of mine. Considering I did my very first stand-up comedy show as a guest at San Quentin State prison, I have a bit of a soft spot for that type of work, even if it's just for nostalgia—a look back at humble beginnings. I cut my comedy teeth working for inmates in locations and environments where, on any particular day or night, I may have been the only one in the chow hall or the auditorium or outside on the dirt in the yard who actually WANTED to be there.

I loved it. Still do.

This Mississippi correctional facility was somewhere I had never been, and I wasn't sure I could find it. It was located way out in a rural location, in the middle of farmlands, ranches, and just plain nothing. Mississippi is one of those states that is densely populated in many areas, which are, in turn, surrounded by thousands of miles of swampland, forest, and uninhabited acreage. When it comes to people, productivity, or poverty, Mississippi is truly a place of haves and have-nots. I was about to do a show for about 800 of the probably never gonna haves.

As I guided my teeny tiny rental car from the Jackson airport, I tried to follow a state map and some handmade notes I had put together. The prison was a few hours away, and I was pushing the speed limit to make the deadline. You see, if you're late for a penitentiary show, there IS no show. This appearance was important to me and I knew I could make a difference to the inmates. If I could only get there on time.

Doing the best I could to follow the map, pay attention to the notes, watch the traffic on the highway, mind the speedometer, and look for signs on the road, my anxiety level was hitting the 100 percent mark. Of course, I found myself lost at some point. I had driven off the main highway and onto a country road that was becoming smaller and narrower the further I followed it. Pulling over to the side, I took a breath and looked out at a 360-degree view. Nothing. Flat, empty space. I started to say a little prayer, asking for guidance. I'm not sure who the patron saint of lost road comics is, so I just prayed to some funny guy in Heaven.

A word or two in my handwritten notes caught my attention. It said, "Follow the signs for Tilden." Right! I needed to go right about three miles back! I can do this, I thought. Looking at my watch, I believed I could get to the prison just before the deadline. If I drove super fast and did not get lost again.

I got lost again.

Following the directions and the map, I ended up on a windy two-lane county road surrounded by nothing but farmland. Frustrated, angry, and scared I wouldn't make it, I pushed the car above seventy miles an hour until I spotted a man working on a fence just off the right side of the road. I slowed down and pulled up to within about seventeen feet of him. I rolled down the passenger side window to ask him a question. That's right, I physically reached over and rolled down the passenger side window. This was an old, very cheap rental car.

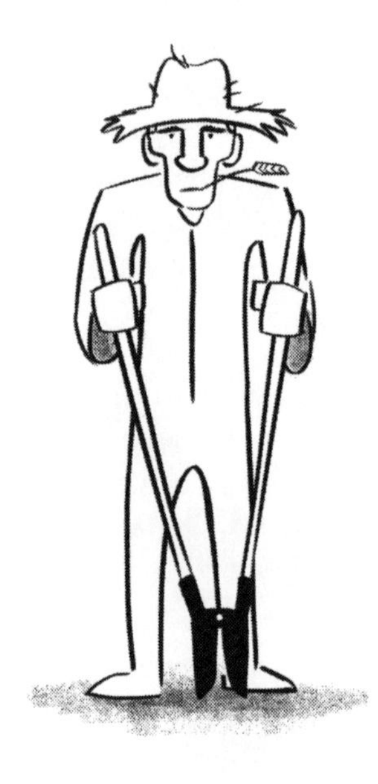

The man I was about to address was clearly a farmer. He was wearing very old, very dirty overalls with no shirt underneath. He could not have weighed more than 140 pounds, and all six feet of him were wiry, tanned, and muscular. He had worked the land with his bare hands for a long, long time. Currently, he was using a post hole digger for part of the fence he was mending. He was slamming it into the ground, pulling out chunks of earth and setting them off to the side in a pile.

"Hey, old-timer! I really need some help. I'm lost, and I need to get to the prison. Do you know the prison? Can I ask for your help with some directions?" He set the post hole digger up against a part of the fence, grabbed a handkerchief from a deep hip pocket on the overalls, took off his straw hat, and wiped his shiny bald head. "Well . . . What you want to do is . . . Go down the road here apiece. Make a left when you see Fred's barn. The prison will be on your right. You can't miss it."

I couldn't believe what I had just heard. Apiece? Who's Fred? I'm not from around here. "Hey, sir . . . Not sure if you understood what I said, but I'm looking for the state prison. I'm a visitor in this area, and I have no idea what you just said. How do I get to the prison?" The farmer looked up at the sky and then back down at the dirt he was so familiar with. He scuffed the toe of his boot around the edge of the hole he was making, and then he said to me: "What you want to do is . . . Go down the road here apiece. Make a left at Fred's barn. Prison will be on your right. You can't miss it."

I thought I was losing my mind, but I was positive I was losing my temper. "Hey buddy, I'm not sure how it works out here, but apiece doesn't mean anything to me, and I never heard of fucking Fred. Are you slow, are you stupid?" The farmer slowly wiped his face and neck and the top of his head. He took a small breath and looked me right in the eyes. He said: "Maybe, but I ain't lost."

I put the car in the drive and slammed on the gas pedal. I was livid. A piece?! Fred?! What the hell was this guy thinking?! I needed to get to the prison, and I had about six minutes to do it. Dammit. What a waste of time that farmer had been! Five seconds later, I saw the sign. On top of a large wooden building was a billboard that read "Fred's Barn." It was huge. And it was only about a two-minute drive from the old farmer's fence.

I made a left.

Almost immediately on my right was the Mississippi prison. I was going to make it on time. In fact, had I not argued with the farmer, I probably would've been here at least five minutes earlier. What a waste of time my questions had been. I thought back to what he had taken the time and patience to say to me:

1. *Down the road apiece*
2. *Left at Fred's barn*
3. *Prison on your right*

His directions had been perfect. I could not miss it. And the show itself? Amazing. Unforgettable. But it almost didn't happen because I knew too much (and not enough) to follow directions.

All I had to do was tell that old guy the whole truth: "I'm afraid right now. I'm totally out of my comfort zone here. I don't know what you're saying to me. Could you be a little more specific for an out of town, rush to judgment, egotistical young know-it-all? Sir?" We don't know until we know. And we can't know if we don't learn to say "I don't know," you know?

STARTING POINT

At twenty-seven years old, I found that I had a little bit of a cocaine problem. At least that's what I told the intake nurse at the Starting Point treatment center in the Hayward Hospital the day I arrived for detox. I was on the verge of losing my truck-driving job, marriage, savings account, and many friends and family. Of course, none of this was anything I would admit to. The truth I knew at the time was that I had a little bit of a cocaine problem. I just wanted to quit the coke, keep all of the stuff I just mentioned, and get back to my life. The 100 percent truth I knew was that this was a minor inconvenience, and I'd like to get it fixed, like a flat tire or a leaky roof.

The doctor who sat me down to interview me regarding my drinking and drug history was a man named Dr. Bromley. I didn't know this at the time, but he was a pioneer in the addiction treatment field. His understanding, wisdom, and experience were far beyond anything I could've imagined and more advanced than most physicians in the United States at that time. I was beyond blessed to have his attention, and I could not have cared less! I just wanted him to fix my little cocaine problem.

I was treating this thirty-day treatment center like a drive-through window. In and out, thank you. Got things to do (badly), people to see (inconsistently), and promises to break (repeatedly).

I didn't know how to say, "I don't know. Will you help me?"

Then I was introduced to Char, my counselor. She was a hardcore, no BS, take no prisoners, street-savvy, professional healer. She was strong and committed and effective and honest. Unfortunately, I was none of the above.

The truth I was willing to tell these people at this point in my life was that I was distracted by cocaine. Everything else in my life would be OK once I quit the drugs. In fact, I wasn't even sure I really needed detox or treatment. Other people in my life were having a hard time with my behavior and attitude, but didn't that mean this was their problem?

I thought I was doing a pretty good job of keeping it all together, and I would tell you that every chance I got. I just had a little cocaine problem.

It turns out that Dr. Bromley and his team, experts that they were, had assigned Char to be my case manager specifically because I had denial and avoidance issues. She could be a perfect teacher for me . . . if I could only start telling her the truth.

Instead of working on my own emotional and mental stuff, I believed that if I looked good enough and sounded good enough, they would treat me like I was healed.

I had what I considered a treatment center prison sentence of twenty-eight days. I decided to use this time as a short vacation from my job. It would give me some necessary distance from my nosy wife, time to get my body in a little bit of shape, and the opportunity to eat all the decent food I could get.

My Teamsters insurance was paying for all of it. How could I not take advantage of this time to let people know how good I was doing? I would listen and learn for four weeks, work on my cocaine problem, and get on with my life. Maybe I could even have a little fun during the process.

The fun went like this: I carried a clipboard around the detox unit. I used it to take notes about what I was hearing in case I needed to use some of that information. Because of the clipboard, occasionally, some new patient, visitor, or family member would approach me and ask me a question as if I was a staff member.

I would not do anything to make them think differently. When they would ask me, "Can you help me please?" I would simply respond, "What do you need?" I guess my emotional insecurity and immaturity were showing, but I could not have told you that at the time. A new patient once said to me, "Do you think that's funny?" I responded, "Every single time."

It got to the point where I was so starved for attention and suffering from what I considered a lack of control of my surroundings that I would walk up to a fellow inpatient, someone I didn't like, and I'd say point-blank, "You know . . . You're not fooling anyone." That person would immediately ask me what I had meant by that. I'd say, "YOU know." And then I'd walk away. If there was a later confrontation, I always had an answer for that too.

My truth at that time was this: I can tell you anything and everything about yourself or someone else, but I was not going to tell anyone about me. I had the mentality that I really didn't like me, and if I took a risk and told you about me, then there would be two of us who didn't like me. Part of me knew this truth. But I wasn't willing to let anyone else in on it. If the healers were so darn good in this place, let them figure it out.

I went to all the groups, showed up for all the head counts, and listened to all the lectures. I got in line when I was supposed to, raised my hand at all the appropriate times, and followed every direction they gave me to the best of my ability or at least a very low level of willingness. I said all the right things at all the right times and survived four weeks of drug and alcohol treatment. I was given the OK to be discharged with consent from the medical and psychological staff. Attaboy!

I was proud of myself, and so were most of my family and friends. But the sad fact was that I had learned very little about myself, them, the nature of my feelings, or what the hell to do about any of those things. My mistake was, because I decided I didn't need any help, I didn't get very much help. Not nearly enough to make a difference.

Less than two weeks after I left the treatment center, I was drunk and doing a lot more cocaine. I had a lot less hope and almost no support, and I was looking at another rock bottom.

MULTIPLE LANGUAGES

If I asked you a question and asked you to tell the truth as your answer, could you do it? And what percentage of that answer would be truthful? Are you capable of telling 100 percent truth every time you answer a question? Let's find out.

How many languages do you speak? That's the question. How many languages do you speak? Many times during a group I'm facilitating, I'll ask this very same question. Invariably, an inmate or a soldier or a residential treatment client will say to me, "One." Sometimes two or three. Rarely does someone tell me they speak five or six languages. But I always ask a second time. "How many languages do you speak?" Answer: "I told you. One!" Or "I told you. Three!" Then I will gently offer them this invitation: "If I ask you a question today, it's not an accusation or an invasion of your privacy. It's so that I can help you better by finding out a little bit more about you. I don't read minds and I don't read your case files, and the staff here doesn't give me any inside information about y'all. I'm trying to help you the best I can with thc truth you're willing to tell me. And sometimes the problem is that we don't know the whole truth, so we get very little help. I'm here to stop that process today. It's simple: more truth, more help. The delicate part for me is whether I wanna raise the level of truth in this room so that I can raise the level of help you're going to receive. I may have to ask you the same question several times in a row. The same exact question!

"How many languages do you speak? Same answer? OK, try this:

"Do you speak sarcasm? Do you speak stubborn? Are you fluent in forgiveness or faith? Do you speak compassion, or do you speak codependent and victim? Do you speak maternal? Do you speak criminal or adolescent or depression or corporate or female or legalese or grieving or selfish? Do you speak slow down and think past your first thought? Do you speak reactionary and insecurity?

"Do you speak patience and calm as we were going through this exercise?

"Now. Let me ask you a question: How many languages do you speak? One hundred percent truth is something for you to tell when it's your turn to answer. But consider all the help you'll receive if you respond with . . .

" 'I speak as many languages as it takes. Hundreds and hundreds of them.'

" 'What language do I need today?'

" 'I don't know, which one would you like?'

" 'Many, many, and I'm willing to learn more.'

"Inquisitive replaces accusatory, and 'listening' becomes another language in and of itself. Am I listening to the universe and the truth it is telling me? Or am I telling it what I want from it? Again!"

I've become fluent in reframing a question, scenario, situation, or challenge as a way to gain insight and solutions so that I have more options to consider when challenged or called to act. So that I don't have to guess. And it all comes from raising the level of truth I tell. And from thinking past my first thought to get to one that works better.

Chapter 6 Wrap-Up

Throughout my entire life and certainly my career, the single greatest liability I possess is the unwillingness to ask for help. When faced with a question now, I remember the two most important sentences in the English language: "I don't know. Can you help me?"

A challenge, a trial, a hurdle. Is it a right or left turn I'm supposed to make? I realize I am allowed to ask questions. Ask questions as opposed to demanding answers or expecting solutions because I'm entitled or selfish or just too lazy to do the work to get the answers. I am responsible for where I am, who I am, and what I need to do. At the end of the day, I've learned a critical lesson. "I don't know. Can you help me?" can become "I do know. I will help you."

Reflection Section:

Examine a situation in life where you did not ask for help when you really needed it. How did that turn out?

Can you remember a time in your recent past when you didn't know enough of the truth to get the help you needed?

Is there a recent memory you have where you learned a lesson because you DID ask for help?

What are you struggling with today, and who will you ask for the help you need?

Chapter 7

Grateful Never Relapses

The ability to appreciate what you have, who you are, what you've learned, and what you can pass on to others is plenty of motivation to get out of bed every morning and thrive. Relapse in this chapter can mean "fail" or "forget" or "coast." These are directions NOT recommended for consistent success and growth.

SUPER SPONSEE

I once sponsored a guy who was an all-star caliber alcoholic in recovery. At fifty-two years of age, he had over twenty years of sobriety and a whole bunch of stuff: a huge new house, a loving wife, two beautiful and intelligent kids, his own business, three or four male sponsees who admired him, and the respect of most of the AA fellowship in his hometown. Basically, he was a rockstar in recovery. Whatever he had lost throughout his drinking career, he had certainly recovered with his sobriety. Oh yeah, one other thing: He happened to be cheating on his wife.

His brand-new girlfriend was only twenty-three years old with a tight, young body and an impressionable mind. She was two months sober, with the face of an angel and a tattoo of the devil on the back of her left shoulder. She was easy to look at and hard to forget.

She was also a newcomer to Alcoholics Anonymous (AA). Dating a newcomer was frowned upon in the Fellowship because it was extremely cruel and considered abusive and predatory. It's known as the thirteenth step. Many newcomers have been ruined or run out of meetings because someone with "time" has come on to them using the tools of AA or the promise of sobriety as an aphrodisiac. As hard as it is to watch as a bystander, it's even harder to survive as the newcomer. It almost never works out for either party, and usually the partner with less sobriety time is devastated. Usually.

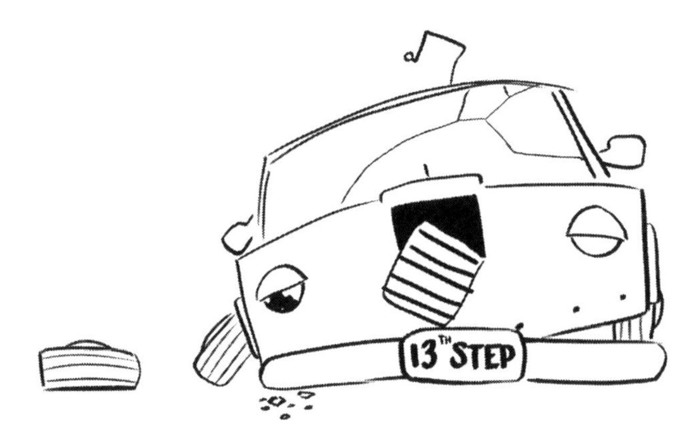

Personally, I did my own dance with the dating of newcomers or the convenient brief sexual dalliance with a woman in recovery who never heard me ask her, "How long have you been sober?" As embarrassing as it is to admit this, I thought the loophole in the "early recovery relationship" thing was that if I didn't ask, I wouldn't know. That way, I'm not breaking any rules. Knowingly.

In truth, I almost always knew what I was doing. That it was wrong. But I knew better. That's what I imagined my cheating sponsee would hear when I talked to him about his current condition: infidelity. Addicted to ego. I changed; why couldn't he? He would have to listen to me.

My own sponsor had been thirteenth-stepped as well. I remember asking him to tell me the story one time. He had only been my sponsor for a couple of months, and I had mentioned to him that I had a new girlfriend and I wanted to learn how to take it slow. "Going slow has never been my strong suit," I said. "Can you help me?"

Steve responded like this: "Here's my experience with going slow. She had a little over a year sober and I had a couple of months. I met her at a recovery dance and we liked each other right away. We had sex that night and moved in together that weekend. We've been together ever since then. Married for over thirty-five years now. That's what I know about taking it slow."

I thought it was one of the best anomaly stories I'd ever heard in my recovery experience. I still think it's funny. Because I know it's true. And they're still together.

My sponsee and I agreed to meet for dinner one night, and I was going to let him have it. He knew he was out of line regarding his marriage vows, and he knew I knew it. A sponsor in AA is like a guide, an interpreter, a translator. Our job is to tell someone who has asked us for help the truth, where it is, and how to get there. Staying there is the responsibility of every recovering alcoholic. As his sponsor, I wasn't willing to work harder on his marriage than he was. I couldn't care more about his family than he did. That's the "tough love" we talk about. It's tough on the ones who give that kind of love. Usually much tougher than it is on the ones who receive that kind of love. I was about to give him a full dose of the toughest love I could dish out.

At dinner, he explained that he was in love with this young girl. That he was infatuated. That he had "Never, ever had feelings like this for anyone before." He was going to leave his wife and kids and move in with this new girlfriend into a trendy downtown upscale apartment.

Why not? He had plenty of money, plenty of time, plenty of recovery, plenty of experience, and plenty of energy for a nice young girl. He had plenty. As I listened to him speak, my resolve to scold him and rip him a new one faded away. He was determined, and his mind had been made up. He never once bothered to check with his interpreter, his guide, or even his God. He was very clear on this point. He was going to do this and give it a try, no matter what.

I decided to tell him what I needed to say to him anyway. "Listen, man. I love you, and so does your family. So do YOUR sponsees. My job has never been to tell you what to do, but I can tell you what NOT to do if you're listening. Don't do this yet. Wait two months and try to work it out with your wife. Clean up one house before you make another one. You do not want to be one of those cliché AA middle-aged males chasing tail, giving up a whole bunch of stuff, including responsibility to other people, only to find out that the tail he was chasing was his own! You're a better man than that. I need you to remember that you're a better man than that."

He put his head down, took a deep breath, brought his head back up, and met my eyes. After a long silence, he said, "I have to do this, Mark."

I said, "You love your wife and your kids and your home, right? You love them, right? You're grateful for all that you have? Grateful for your beautiful family, that loyal and loving wife? Are you, big shot?"

He whispered, "Not enough to STAY with them."

The next morning, he moved out of the new house and into the new apartment.

I had a hard time speaking to him after that. I didn't fire him as a sponsee. I was told that AA sponsors don't do that. An old-timer at a meeting said, "Sponsees fire themselves. They'll do it for you." So I waited for this guy to do his own work and shoot himself in the foot. Then I'd try to be available

when he came back to his senses and see what we could do about patching things up with his wife and family. He was taking a detour from his sane and sober life and a vacation from his true feelings or whatever else he was calling it, and I would just have to be patient. He was experienced and smart, and I knew sooner or later he would figure out that he made the wrong move, let the girlfriend down gently, and go back to reality.

What actually happened was much different. After a few months of living together, the girlfriend left HIM. She decided to date someone else in recovery her own age. Some young guy with big biceps and tattoos and a fast Harley Davidson. The new guy had no money, only a few of his own teeth, and no job that anybody knew about. But hey, that's love.

No one saw it ending this way, especially my sponsee. He was devastated and completely humiliated. The new, young, barely sober girlfriend dumped the recovery superstar for some newcomer nobody? What the hell was that? I called Mr. Wonderful, got his voicemail, and left a message: "Hey, brother. Heard you might've taken a gut punch recently, and I'd like to help. I'm always here for you, and you can call anytime you're ready. We will get past this, man."

He never called back. Instead, I received a call from his wife, who had come home to the new house they used to share and found his body hanging in the garage. He had killed himself that morning while she was at work, knowing she would probably be the one to find him. No one—absolutely no one—saw this one coming.

I couldn't breathe after I hung up the phone. I drove over there to talk to her and the kids. His shame and guilt had consumed him. Having been suicidal myself at one point, I could almost imagine what he was feeling as he stepped into the noose.

There really are no words for the family that could help in a situation like this, but I would give my best possible effort for as long as they needed me to be there. And I was absolutely positive about the one thing I could personally take away from the experience: In recovery, you're either grateful or greedy. You can't be both, and there's no third choice. Grateful never gives up, goes back, or loses. Greed never helps anyone, no matter what they have or get in the process.

I belong to a fellowship that's addicted to, obsessed with, or distracted by chemicals. Ego is a chemical too. Both my sponsee and I were guilty of feeding our own. He wouldn't give up the instinctual drive that males have been dealing with since the dawn of time, even for a devoted wife and a lifestyle that he worked very hard to earn and make available to his offspring.

I would have a hard time forgiving myself for thinking that what I knew and what I said to him could change anything. I wasn't sure whose arrogance was worse at this point: mine or his. We were both going to have to pay the price for being cocky and impatient.

WENDOVER DRUNK

Early on in my comedy career, there were many one-nighters, motel rooms, and rest areas along the highway. There were lousy gigs, small crowds, tight money, and bad comedians. How I managed to survive all of this . . . well, that's probably a whole 'nother book. Maybe I'll write that one next. The bottom line is that I was grateful to do something I had dreamed about LONG before I was willing to do anything about doing it. You follow?

1989–90

One of the jobs I had after I first got clean was working for a company called Klassen Tractor. They did paving, grading, road building, house pad construction, and anything to do with moving earth from one place to another. They had heavy equipment, water trucks, huge loaders, and semis. They also had their hands in drag racing as a hobby. Lots of money, motors, and manpower.

The Klassen brothers were successful and well-liked in the industry. I went to work for them, slinging gravel. I had a strong work ethic, a quick shovel, and an even quicker and stronger mouth. From 7 a.m. until dark, my job was to throw shovel-loads of gravel onto a dirt path or roadway. Every once in a while, I would dig out a hole or fill one in . . . with the same shovel.

For a couple of months, I shoveled this way and that. I wrote, rehearsed, and practiced my comedy routine in the mirror of a small bedroom

I was renting inside a house up in the Santa Cruz mountains. My roommate, Don Nofrey, was another sober guy who owned the house and built and sold motorcycles for a living.

As I dragged my tired rear end home at the end of a long day, he would always ask me, "You still shoveling gravel, Superstar?"

I'd always reply, "Yeah, but someday I'm gonna do comedy. You'll see." And every day while I was doing that job, I had a routine. Each time the empty shovel hit the pile of gravel, I would say out loud, "Damn, I want to do comedy! (Scoop) Damn, I want to do comedy! (Scoop) Damn, I want to do comedy!"

I did that job for a couple more months before I finally got the opportunity to do some comedy on the road. Really horrible, flat-bottom-boat booze cruise ships, crappy one-nighters, and D-room comedy clubs were all that were available to the brand-new guy from Santa Cruz, California. This is how comedians got started back then. You worked on your road legs and swallowed the many miles to earn your stage time. Huge, hearty helpings of humble pie. That's just how it was.

Then I signed up for my first road tour. It was a week in Oregon, then Washington, then Idaho, then Montana, then Utah, then Nevada. A full six-week tour doing five or six shows a week at a rate of $200 a night! I was going to make about $7,000 doing stand-up. It was my first real foray into professional comedy. I could not have been happier, and I practically cried in disbelief!

The tour was atrocious.

And my comedy wasn't much better.

Because of my naïveté, I underestimated the power of being homesick for the mountains and isolated from my support system. I didn't know just how tough the road could be. As a result, I was exhausted, lonely, grumpy, and disappointed.

Then there was that night in Wendover, Nevada.

The Red Garter Casino was a one-nighter, once a week on Wednesdays. The casino had a wobbly plywood stage in one corner of a showroom full of slot machines. Fifteen or twenty chairs were facing the plywood corner with a single spotlight stuck in the ceiling overhead. Along each wall, extending from that corner, were slot machines and barstools.

The entire place was loud, smoky, and poorly lit. It was truly a depressing place, especially when I figured out what the one-hour comedy show was all about. I was a sixty-minute distraction for the poor patrons who had run out of money and were nursing their last free drink from the casino—thus, the fifteen or twenty chairs facing the stage. And to make matters worse, there were only about eight people in those fifteen or twenty chairs. I might as well have been the executioner at the gallows. An ugly scene; no one was happy.

As I walked up to the mic that night, I noticed a woman playing two slot machines at the very edge of the stage to my immediate left. She used one arm for each machine, cradled the bucket of coins between her legs, and sucked on a long cigarette. She had to be close to seventy years old and gave me a death stare as I began to speak.

"Hey, everybody. I'm Mark Lundholm, and I'm from California. And like every one of you tonight, I don't gamble anymore either."

I thought it was a funny opening line until I realized that I was the one who had quit voluntarily. So I continued: "I used to drink quite a bit too, but my cocaine habit cured me of that. You have to have priorities, darn it."

Not a sound from the audience . . . except for the slot machine lady. She blinked through the smoky clouds she made in front of her face—never stopping pulling the two handles—and yelled: "Why don't you shut up! (Cough) When are you going to shut up? Why doesn't somebody shut this guy up? (Cough, cough) I'm trying to play here. Can someone SHUT HIM UP?"

Grateful as I was to finally be doing comedy for a living . . . my first thought was, "Damn, I wish I was shoveling gravel right now."

On another night, this situation may have been enough to entice me into drinking or gambling or both. Luckily, I had a second or third or fifteenth thought. One that brought me back from the edge of frustrated, irritated, and isolated . . . to grateful. Grateful I was following a passion.

THIS DAY

When my son, Grayson, was first learning to speak, Julee and I decided that we would take our time with him. We would speak slowly and clearly and often. Verbose, chatty, and wordy are all words that could've described our household—all day, every day. Talk talk talk talk talk. Never at a loss for words, we tried to raise that boy with at least the freedom of speech.

More than anything else, his mother and I had learned from our own childhood that kids needed to know they had a voice. That they could be heard. That Mom and Dad were listening. It gave us both hope that maybe, just maybe, he wouldn't grow up with some of the same low self-esteem issues we had.

For a while, we handled it pretty well. At some point, however, we realized we may have created a monster. Grayson learned to speak early and often. Lots of words. He had questions and comments and sayings and ways of speaking that were often intriguing and annoying at the same time. Julee used to say to me: "Oh my dear lord. He is just like a little YOU!" And she wasn't saying that in a cute, complimentary way.

Grayson would often pop into a room unannounced and ask, "Ready, guys? Mom? Dad? Ready guys? OK, be right back then."

Or

"What is up, guys? Wanna see somethin', guys?"

Or

"Whoooooooo's hungry? How about some food for the dude?" OK, that one he got from his dad.

But he did have lots of other unique and original ways and words to describe the life around him and his perceptions of all of it. His mother and I have both marveled at the combination of simplicity and early eloquence in his delivery.

When he was very young, he asked me to look at the rain on the car windshield. He said, "It's like a ballet of water falling out of the sky." I snapped my neck to look back at him and had to remind myself he was five years old. First thought wrong? "How the hell am I going to be smart enough to raise this kid?"

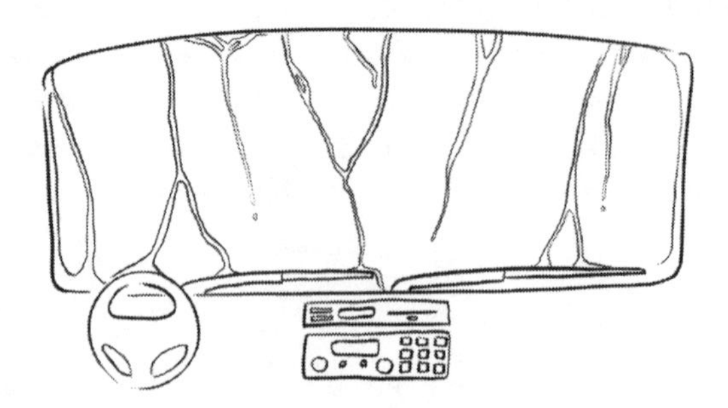

One example was a true classic. And it was all his. As a young kid, he never said the word "today." Never. He would always say, "This day."

No matter what his mother and I tried, no matter how many ways we said it, he would always say "this day" instead of "today." For a while, I wondered if he was impaired somehow, but everything else about language he seemed to pick up immediately. But this was just weird. I would say to him, "Today for lunch we are having mac and cheese, Mr. Man." Or, "Hey, bug (short for love bug), we get to go swimming today!" He would respond, "This day, Dad? We can swim this day then?" Or "What's for dinner this day, Dad?" I actually remember being irritated at times, like my kid wasn't listening. Every single time we used the word today, he heard "this day."

One particular evening on the road, while I was trying to get to sleep at the hotel, I heard what he was actually saying to me. He was teaching me that today is really all we have. This day is the present. A gift. We can only exist in this one day: today. Even if we have lived a long time, all we really have is today.

I remember laying in bed thinking, "I've had a Friday before. I've had a June 22nd before. In fact, I've had tons of Fridays and lots of June 22nds before. But I have never ever in my life had THIS day." I was shocked at the PURITY I had overlooked for the past couple of years of Grayson's life.

He was so right, and I had been focused on how wrong he was at saying the word 'today.' What a beautifully perfect way to look at the world. Grateful for this day. I still hear his voice as I say those words. "This day, Dad!"

By the time he was nine or ten years old, he was saying the word "today" regularly. He had become one of the rest of us and left that part of his childhood behind. That perfect past of a child's early life where they see and hear things differently than those of us who have thickened our skin and crusted over after a while. It happens to everyone sooner or later. But I will still tell the story in group and sometimes in a motivational talk. The time where, early in his life, my son would talk about and feel excitement for "this day." He was energetic and grateful for this day. Not a bad way to live, really.

Chapter 7 Wrap-Up

This day . . . I am grateful to know all of the following: The entire time I've been sober, I've been in some form of service. Jails and prisons, shelters, detoxes, halfway houses, Salvation Army residences, sober living environments, women's shelters, whether recognized, publicized or private. I've worked with people who suffer from addiction, are related to an addict or alcoholic, have some kind of mental illness they struggle with, or have experienced abuse in their past. I go because I owe! It has been a joy to do this kind of work, and it's been a lesson. Gratitude is a guarantee. Service to others becomes a true sense of self, and complacency is gratitude without service.

Pro bono is a Latin phrase meaning "for good." Good can refer to the work, the recipient, or me. No one loses in that equation. I'm grateful for that, too.

Reflection Section:

Make a list of five things you are grateful for today.

Describe a specific situation in your life when you were not grateful for what was happening at the time but discovered gratitude for the situation later?

One of the most difficult things to do is find gratitude in something negative, challenging, or painful. Can you think of an example of this in your recent past?

Chapter 8

Different Precedes Better

There is an old saying: "You are putting the cart before the horse." It makes me laugh now because I've never had either one of those things. But I've done that exact thing in hundreds of situations. I wanted to be better, do better, feel better without doing anything differently. Oh sure, it's funny NOW!

LORAIN COUNTY LADIES

A few years back, maybe 2010 or 2011, I performed in the women's unit of the Lorain County Jail near Cleveland, Ohio. It was an annual visit that I have been making since the mid-1990s. Lorain County at one time had the single highest death rate from opiates per capita in the United States. They also had a lot of alcoholics and drug addicts locked up in their county system.

Having performed more than 500 shows, for hundreds of thousands of inmates, in several hundred different prisons in this country, it's my humble opinion that over ninety percent of incarcerated individuals have a personal history or family history of chemical, physical, and psychological abuse. As depressing as this may sound, Lorain County Jail was one of my favorite visits. From the hospitality they showed me—both inmates and staff—I think it was also one of their favorite days on the unit. They kept asking me back each year, and I kept showing up. That's the definition of a committed relationship, isn't it? Anyway, we were dating.

My visits were always on a weekday and part of a five-day residency gig I did in Cleveland every year. I would perform ten or eleven times in those five days. Everything from a golf tournament to a large theater for a general audience to a high school, several treatment centers, and, of course, two or three jails and Grafton Prison. It was an exhausting schedule, but even in comedy, the saying applies, "no pain, no gain." I would survive that week with the same mechanism and tools I used to stay sober and on the right track as a father and a successful performer: one day at a time. Which brings me back to the Lorain County Jail women's unit.

On this visit, as always, I walked through the front door of the reception area, checked in with the sheriff at the window, traded my California driver's license for a visitor's badge, signed the hostage waiver, asked for my contact there (a lieutenant who was a huge fan, a disciplined professional, and a very caring officer of the law), and allowed myself to be escorted through the metal detector and up to the sallyport. This was always one of my favorite parts of any prison or jail visit. There's a sound that an automatic metal lock makes that resembles nothing else on earth. It is a sudden and extremely loud clang! It signifies the locking out of the exterior world and the locked-in and locked-down world of incarceration. For me, it is exhilarating and disturbing at the same time.

If you've ever been an inmate or a visitor in an institution, the sound may become familiar but never comfortable. That sound can represent a loss of freedom and a loss of hope. In the reverse direction, it signifies the new beginning of both of those things. But it is a sound you never get used to, and you never forget. Clang!!! I hate it and I love it.

The comedy show was always in the very small, very clean indoor basketball gym. The two sheriffs who escorted me and my favorite lieutenant always arrived first. They then waited for the female inmates to be escorted from their pods to the gym. It's a process known as "movement."

Anywhere between twenty and fifty women were allowed to attend the show. They had to have decent behavior for the few days prior to my arrival, and if all the women in all the pods were well-behaved, because of the limited space and the security issues, the correctional officers had a lottery system to determine which women got to see the show. It was a nice problem for me to have. It meant that the inmates actually wanted to come and see the performance. Trust me, that's better than doing a show in a prison or jail where nobody wants to be sitting in that room with me. Occasionally I still do one of those shows as well. I can always turn an audience around, but it's so much nicer when they are already willing to laugh. These women were.

I got into the material, and everything was going smoothly. We were laughing pretty hard. It was time for me to bring the ladies to a screeching halt and use that silence and pause in the proceedings to deliver them a message. This is one of the tools of the trade it took me several years to learn how to do. An audience can only laugh really HARD for about twenty minutes, then they need a rest for a couple of minutes to catch their breath. If you don't let them have that couple of minutes to breathe and shift and adjust in their seats, they won't be with you for the full sixty minutes. It's a lot like aerobics. It's possible to push a group so hard that they'll quit on you, not because they want to but because they just can't keep up with you. And in Lorain County, I always did a ninety-minute show! We needed to pace ourselves, or it was gonna be a massacre.

"Every time I work at a female institution, there's always the innocent inmate. Where is that lady today?" I asked the group.

One of the women answered, "Right here, sir. I really didn't do it this time." There was substantial laughter from the other women in the room.

"This time," I responded. "And before?"

The inmate joked: "Oh, guilty as hell! The other time!" A much bigger laugh from the other women in the room.

I laughed as well, took a breath, and said very calmly, "What if they locked you up for everything you really DID do? What if life were FAIR, and you had to answer for every crime you DID commit? I'm not judgin', I'm just sayin'."

Sudden silence. Then just as quickly, every inmate in the room shook their head, made some kind of low guttural sound, or said, "Damn," or "No," or "Lord help me," or "I'd be doin' life." They all immediately understood what I was trying to say.

A lot of people on this planet would have to admit that if we had been given justice instead of mercy, the price we'd have had to pay would be much higher.

While I had their full attention, I asked them another question. "How fair do you think it is that our families also have to pay the price for what each one of us has done? The distance and loss and shame? How expensive is it to be related to one of us? What do you think, my innocent friend? How does your mom feel about all of this?"

"Why don't you ask her yourself?" she said. "She sittin' two rows behind me." I felt like I'd been punched right in the chest. Speechless. Affected. This was a first for me. Mom and daughter in the same jail on the same exact day that I was visiting. I took a couple of deep breaths and then looked to the row where Mom was slowly nodding her head. "Mom? Got to be tough to be sitting in this very room with your own daughter, don't you think?"

The inmate's mom replied, "Why don't you ask my mom? She's right up there in the front."

Not a sound in the room. My eyes drifted to the front row, to the furthest seat on the right, closest to the door they had all come through. There, a much older woman, drawn and thin and gray, stared out the small window of the gym door. She never met my eyes. Not even once. Just gazed sadly at a future she didn't have and a past she couldn't change. I had no idea what to say next. So I looked at the granddaughter and asked, "Do you have a daughter?"

She nodded. "Yes I do. She's with child services right now, but I'm going to get her back. For sure. I'm gonna get her back."

I said, "And how are you going to do that?"

She said, "I'm going to do things different than my mother and her mother did. Whatever it takes to be different than them. That's gonna be me."

I don't know if that's the way it went for her after I left that day, but I've never forgotten the feeling I had, the message I received, and the power of that particular visit as I stored it away in my skull. If nothing changes, nothing changes. The addiction cycle, the jail visits, the abuse, the unhappy endings . . . it continues as long as we allow it to. Dysfunctional becomes functional only if we do something different than the generations before us. Something better.

DAMON'S DAY

I had been doing volunteer standup comedy for five or six years in plenty of incarcerated environments: prisons, jails, male- and female- correctional facilities. For long-termers, short-timers. I even volunteered at some work release farms where they allowed inmates to work outside in the community during the day and then come back to the institution to sleep at night. This was always some of my favorite comedy work, and most of the time, it seemed that that work was appreciated.

I was also doing standup as a professional, but the clubs and one-nighters, even when I got paid, didn't fill me up the way that the pro bono places did. I guess that's why they say doing good is its own reward. In that respect, comedy had made me a believer for many years.

And then I was invited to appear at a juvenile hall.

My buddy Richard, a counselor at the juvenile correctional facility in Martinez, California, invited me to speak to a group of male inmates aged thirteen to seventeen years. There were minor-aged offenders and major league criminals.

The facility had a census of fifteen inmates the day I had agreed to show up. Richard had asked me to do twenty minutes of standup comedy and then follow up with no more than ten minutes of voluntary questions and answers. He reminded me that the attention span of teenagers—especially ones who had trust issues, ADHD, and abuse in their history—didn't make for a very welcoming and patient audience. I had no idea how accurate that statement was.

These kids knew I was coming. Richard had told them that a very funny professional standup comedian was going to come and talk to them for half an hour. Even worse, he had told them that I didn't take crap from people. I was used to working with adult inmates, so I could handle anything these kids threw at me.

He told them, "He's good. But if you mess with him, he'll eat you up." Wonderful. Exactly what you do not want to do with abandoned kids who have been threatened their entire lives: punch them in the face with an ultimatum. You might as well challenge them to a duel. Nasty attitudes at fifty paces!

In early November, the weather in northern California was chilly and damp. I showed up that morning at about 9:45. Richard met me in the lobby and told me how the show was going to go: The kids would be transferred from the Rec Room to the Assembly Hall, and I would begin the presentation at 10 a.m. At 10:30, the officers would do a headcount of the inmates, and then the kids would be sent to lunch. I would be free to leave at that point. He requested that the presentation be rated PG-13 and that I avoid any obviously toxic topics: sex, murder, abuse, hatred for the police, and any mention of violence or weapons. "No problem," I said. "I think I've got exactly what they need." Well, I thought I did.

As I entered the Assembly Hall, I looked through a huge plate-glass window leading into the other room: a recreational area where the kids were playing ping pong, dominoes, or basketball. As I watched the kids doing their thing, every one of them was also watching me. And one-by-one they started filing into the Assembly Hall, grabbing whatever seat they wanted.

I was astounded at how young they were. I knew their surroundings and alleged crimes, but these were just boys. It made me sad and angry. Why the hell is it necessary to have "kid prisons"?

They started the show without me.

Before I even walked to the head of the room to address them, the jeering and cheering began. Catcalls, wolf whistles, raspberries, and a slew of commentary came flying at me: "Boo! Boo! How did you get in here?" "Somebody take the janitor back to his closet" "Hey everybody, look, it's Eddie Murphy!"

One of the kids, the smallest of the bunch, had the best weapons in the arsenal: He was fast, funny, and never wasted a single word.

"Hey, funny man. You funny? You look funny, but that don't mean you be funny. You best be funny up in here, funny man."

"Hey, clown boy. Is that a haircut or a punishment?"

"That's a nice leather jacket you wearing. But you won't be wearing it long because I'm gonna be taking it from you, funny man. It don't fit me right

now, but it will when I grow into it. Because you won't be having it anymore."

"Are you a faggot? You look like a faggot! Pretty soon, I'll have you crying like a faggot."

Damn. My first fifty thoughts were wrong! I truly wanted to hurt somebody. Not only that, but my heart started to race, my blood started to boil, and my head started to pound out some ideas about how to get back at this little son of a . . . criminal. This damn kid had taken fifteen shots at me already, and I hadn't even opened my mouth to speak. Yet.

Several of the thoughts I had were how to snap this kid's neck while shortening his life and weakening his resolve at the same time. He was a little, skinny, short, Chris-Rock-looking loudmouth punk. And so far, he had put me on the canvas without me throwing a single punch in his direction. I'd be damned if this kid was going to win this battle. After all, I was a professional. I thought about the many ways I could get to him, the many things I could say to him, and the verbal abuse I could bury him with.

And then I remembered the San Quentin show.

I looked the little guy right in the eye, tilted my head toward the ceiling, and planted my feet on the floor. I didn't move them again for a full thirty seconds while I began to breathe in and out. In . . . And out . . . In . . . And out. And all that time, I was running my tongue along the inside of my teeth, counting them as I went. Yep, there were still thirty of them in there. I counted every single one of them while I breathed and concentrated on my feet and the stable balance all of this provided me. Then I started my show.

I made a few jokes about smoking weed and growing up in Oakland as a not-so-tough, very young, skinny white guy who was pretty quick with his language but a little short on courage. I made jokes about how abusive my family was, how much it hurt my feelings, and how it made me defensively funny. I made fun of the staff, the jail food, the luxurious accommodations, and a whole bunch of other things I knew these young men understood. Jokes about where they lived. Stories about what they had seen. Tales about what they had endured. Using myself and my life as a blunt instrument, I whittled away at their thick crocodile skin and their many layers of unnecessary armor. Finally, they started to quiet down. And laugh. Even the little thug life wanna-be Chris-Rock-looking kid.

Only once more did I hear him say, "That's funny, but still not as funny as me, clown boy!" And just five or six minutes into the show, I had them. I had them all. I had the inmates, I had the staff and teachers, and I had the guards.

Because I remembered dealing with the big guy in the front row at San Quentin in 1988 and how much that had cost me that day, I decided to try something a little different. I decided not to react to the little guy here (I found out later his name was Damon) no matter what he said or how fast and hard he came at me. Do it differently, maybe it's better? I wasn't sure it would work, but I definitely knew what did not work!

During the remainder of the twenty-minute comedy set, I watched a transformation in the room take place. I watched these young men go from irritated, defensive animals to young boys, with howls of laughter and genuine appreciation for someone reaching out to them. I watched them grab each other around the neck and squeak with laughter. I watched them throw their heads back, trying to breathe so they could laugh some more. I watched them lean forward as their guts emptied and the air left their lungs. I watched them punch each other in appreciation. "Hey, I got that joke, too!" I watched them turn from a gang of separate legal offenders into a single unified benign force. Willingly. Playfully.

As I closed up, I said to them, "Well, my time is up here, but I promised Richard I'd take a few questions if you have some. If not, it's been fun, and thank you for letting me work for you."

Only one hand went in the air to ask a question. Guess who it belonged to? Guess! That's right. Damon. My First Thought Wrong: Pretend you don't see him raise his hand. Ignore that kid before he goes right back to slamming his wits into you. Run while you still have your leather jacket! You're done. Run. Go.

And then I thought, I told them I would take some questions, and I have this one little guy holding me accountable. I said to Damon, "Yes sir, question?"

"Yeah. Will you come BACK sometime?"

I was floored. I was numb.

I was in awe.

"Well . . . Sure . . . Yeah, I'd love to come back." And then I started to cry. Just a little bit, but they saw. Damon saw.

"Are you crying, faggot? Look at you cry. I knew you were a faggot. Look at you crying!"

I responded, "I'm sorry for my reaction, but you touched me."

Damon quickly retorted, "I didn't touch you. Don't you be talking about touching in here. Ain't nobody touching nobody."

"No, I meant you touched a part of my heart when you asked me to come back."

Damon said, "Well . . . It's 'cause you funny."

"So are you, my young friend," I replied. "So are you."

Damon yelled, "I know that, dumbass! I don't need you to tell me I'm funny. Already know it!"

"My bad," I said. "I know you are, and yes I'll come back."

And I did go back. After the holiday season had passed and the comedy gigs—which are many and diverse during the December season—had calmed down, I went back to the Martinez Juvenile Detention Center to do another short comedy performance. And I don't mind admitting that I was pretty excited to do so. I couldn't wait to see how everybody had grown and thrived during Christmas and New Year's. Being an ex-felon, I knew the holidays were some of the brightest times of the year. Even when I was locked up.

I went through the usual pat-down, metal detector, shoes off, check your pulse, under your tongue, all the yadda yadda of being screened before I arrived in the lobby and the sallyport. And I saw my buddy, Richard. "My brother!"

I greeted him, "What is up with you and yours and ours and theirs!" I was laying it on thick because I was very upbeat and a little hyper to start the show. I was feeling so good about what I had done here last time, I wanted to recreate that for everybody, and I knew I could.

I said, "Can I see my buddy? Where is Damon? Where is my little man?"

Richard didn't respond right away, then he said, "Oh, Damon won't be here. Damon went home on a pass for his birthday, and he was killed. His father beat him to death with a baseball bat. The bat was a birthday gift from his mother. I'm sorry, brother. I didn't know how else to tell you."

I couldn't breathe. My brain felt like it was frozen. I couldn't breathe, and I couldn't move. I couldn't blink. I wanted Richard to repeat what he just said, but I knew I'd heard it right the first time. Damon was killed by his dad.

With a bat. Period.

First thought? I want to hurt that dad. I want to kill that dad because I've known that dad. Second thought? I loved that kid. I loved that kid because I KNEW that kid, and I've been that kid. Hell, I'm STILL that kid!

As I listened to Richard fill me in on the details. That Damon's mom was destroyed. That she lost her husband and son in a single moment. That as the cops threw the dad in the backseat of a cop car, they asked him, "Why would you do that? Why would you kill your boy?" And dad had answered, "That kid could never shut up. The kid could never shut his mouth!"

And I thought quietly to myself, "Yes, he could. He could be quiet. He could shut his mouth. In fact, he could be gentle and hospitable and warm and attentive and complimentary and funny. He could have done a lot of things. He could have been a lot of things, had he survived somebody else's First Thought Wrong."

I still think about Damon. Every time someone tries to heckle me or take a verbal shot at me or my character or upbringing or my mother or some other target they think will get me to engage. I take a little peek up toward the sky. I think, "Thanks little fella, for reminding me to be different. And for what you taught me."

In thirty minutes, just thirty minutes, he taught me something that I've used for the rest of my life. He taught me that it's the difference between us that allows us to make a difference around us. I was with that kid for thirty minutes, and he affected me forever. And now he's affected you. Thirty minutes.

Imagine what we could do with a whole day.

Chapter 8 Wrap-Up

After many, many years, it's been my experience that life is literally made up of one decision at a time. And if I'm truly keeping it super simple here, I'll say it like this:

One choice works, and one doesn't. These days I choose the one that works. Or I don't choose the one that doesn't work and (based on experience) my next choice is healthier. The newly discovered and different choice produces a better outcome.

I cannot count the times in my life when I wanted to do something better, yet I refused to do anything differently. That makes me laugh reading what I just wrote. If I want a better result, I have to take a different action, choose a different behavior, or make a different choice. Sound better? I'm sure it sounds different.

Reflection Section:

What practice or behavior have you changed because it wasn't working? What did you do differently?

How different are you today compared to one year ago? What significant changes have you made in that year?

If you had a magic wand and could change two things about yourself today, right this minute, what would those two things be? Can you make those two changes without asking for help?

Chapter 9

If You Have a Gift, You Have to Give

I recently heard a line from a fantastic film, A Bronx Tale. Something to the effect of "the saddest thing in life is wasted talent." After many years of wasting my own talent, I agree.

True recovery is a product of passion, using what the universe gave you as a gift given BACK TO the universe. What a concept.

GROCERY GUY

I grew up in the grocery business. My dad had a small mom-and-pop store in San Leandro, California, and my mother and the five of us kids made six wonderful employees for my father.

When I was five years old, I learned how to bag groceries, stack up old cartons of Coke bottles, sweep the back room, throw out the garbage from the produce department, clean out the meat locker, and restock the groceries on the shelves. When I was about fifteen, there was nothing under the roof of a grocery store I could not do. At eighteen, I was already a journeyman clerk in the Grocery Workers' Union.

So in 1978, while I pretended to attend college classes at San Jose State University, I got a job at Food Villa in the Pruneyard in Campbell. It turned out to be the perfect playground for a guy who had all the grocery store knowledge in the world, tons of energy, youth to spare, an almost lethal knowledge of human behavior, and the gift of gab! Oh, yeah, and I was funny.

Now, being funny is like every other talent or tool we possess, but we need to learn the difference between using humor as a shield and using it to connect. If I'm using my sense of humor to separate me from intimacy or reality or getting to the truth of something, it's a shield, a barrier. On the other hand, if I use comedy as a tool or connection point or to illustrate truth or intimacy, it becomes a shelter to protect integrity, connection, myself, my family, and everyone I care about. I mean, are the gifts we possess preventing something or providing something? Am I pushing people away or inviting them in?

Shield? Or connection?

The Food Villa supermarket turned out to be basic training for a soldier of standup comedy, and while I have to admit that I didn't always do a good job of being a grocery clerk, my improv skills and crowd work banter were honed to a very fine, razor-sharp edge. It was like having my own show! There were hundreds of moments like these:

An announcement I made over the store loudspeaker one Saturday morning at about 8 a.m. "Attention Food Villa shoppers. For the next sixty minutes, all the ladies working in our bakery department will be naked from the waist up! That's right, folks. There's a half-off sale in the bakery at Food Villa. Have a nice weekend."

And this one:

We used to sell all the gossip rag mix: The Enquirer, The Daily Mail, Star, etcetera. A certain part of our clientele at the grocery store found them entertaining. To me, they were just irritating, so when a customer purchased one of these papers, I would charge that customer one extra dollar. I called it "idiot tax." The magazine was only about twenty-five cents, but I charged them the extra dollar anyway.

Most of these customers never noticed, but if they did and they asked me, "What's the dollar on my sales receipt?" I would always tell them the truth. "Oh, that there is an idiot tax. You bought an Enquirer magazine, right?" The customer might say, "Well, yes. Yes I did." And I'd respond, "Right, you're an idiot."

I made several people angry with that move, but I don't remember ever having to return a single dollar. And what's funny to me is that most people never noticed the tax at all. Maybe because they were idiots?

And then there was this one:

Food Villa used to cash payroll checks on Fridays. Some customers had a check-cashing card issued by our store, and it allowed them to write checks for groceries or receive cash for their paycheck. One customer in particular would come in on payday, toss his check onto the counter without saying a word, check still folded up from being in his pocket, and expect to cash the check without so much as saying hello. He did that every week! Until he tried it at my check stand.

That day, I had a long line at my register, and I was working at my usual lightning-fast pace. I really was an excellent employee—when I kept my mouth shut. So here comes the guy.

Tossing his folded-up Friday check on the counter in front of me, Mr. Warmth says:

"Hurry up and cash this thing, and I want all big bills. Understand?"

I looked into the man's face, then down at the check, then back up again at the man's face. I took my left hand and, using my forefinger and my thumb, made a backward "C." Then, using my right hand, I took my forefinger and my thumb and made the letter "C." In between the two Cs was about three inches of empty space. As he stared at the rectangular shape I had made, I said, "You know, all United States bills are exactly the same size. If you want bigger bills, you may have to go to a different country."

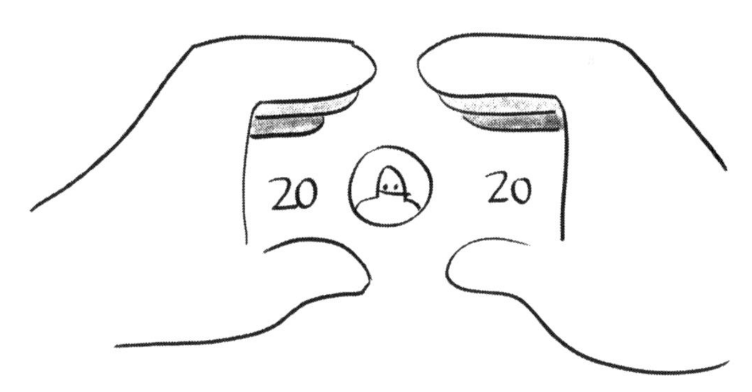

Stunned as he was, it didn't take him very long to let me know what he thought about what I had said. "Hey, Henny Youngman, cash that check or I'll go up and speak to the manager!"

I said, "Well, if you're going to speak to the manager, you're gonna have to wait a while; he doesn't like people to wake him up during his afternoon nap. And that's right now. You could wait, I guess."

The customer responded, "What in the Sam Hell is wrong with you, boy?"

I replied, "How much time do you have?"

This one actually got me fired.

I can't say that I've ever hated many things in my life. Maybe myself for a bit and social or racial injustices that I have witnessed. And certainly bullying or physical abuse, especially when I've seen it firsthand. Hate that stuff. But at Food Villa, my pet peeve, my very least favorite thing in the entire universe, would have been when customers complained needlessly. Like when a gentleman wanted to purchase a fifty-dollar bottle of California Merlot.

Food Villa was widely known for its fantastic specialty cuts of meat, the freshest produce, an extensive wine selection, and gourmet liquor items. The South Bascom Avenue and Willow Glen residential area was a relatively affluent neighborhood. And as everybody knows, affluence affords those folks special privileges on multiple levels. Just ask them, like the Merlot man.

After reaching my check stand counter, he immediately piped up with: "Hey, I heard this wine is especially good. But fifty effing dollars? Ain't no bottle of wine worth fifty bucks, know what I'm saying?"

"Oh, right. I hear you, man," I replied.

And then I took the Merlot bottle off the counter and stashed it behind my cash register. "I'll put it back later."

Looking extremely surprised and a tad worried, the customer said, "Hey, what are you doing? That's my bottle."

"No. Not anymore it isn't," I responded. "Didn't sound like you wanted it. I'll take it from here."

The customer sputtered, "You can't do that! I want that one!"

I replied, "Sure didn't sound like you wanted it. In fact, it seems to me that you were complaining about paying fifty bucks for it. See, here's how it works in MY check stand: You give me the fifty bucks, and you buy the wine. Because that's the price of the wine. Or you complain about the price of the wine, I take the bottle, you keep your fifty bucks and nobody loses anything, including their temper. What I'm trying to tell you is this: If you whine about the wine, you don't get the wine. If you don't whine about the wine, I'm fine with selling you the wine. For fifty bucks. BUT, at this check stand, with this clerk, there are no 'bitch and buy' privileges. Understand, Mr. Merlot expert?"

The gentleman left the store without another word and is probably still holding his breath. About thirty minutes later, I looked up from my check stand counter and saw the manager standing about five feet away from me. He said, "Mark, I just got a phone call from a heavy breather who says we owe him a bottle of Merlot. Do you know anything about that?"

Some of my greatest gifts started out as a weapon, armor. I thought

I needed to shield my insecurities from everyone else. Humor is like a scalpel; it is sharp and cuts deeply. I can be a surgeon or a slasher. I can butcher something or buoy someone. But, like every other tool I possess, it took a while to learn how and when to use it correctly.

MR. YAKOV SMIRNOFF

From 1992 to about 1995, I wrote jokes, stories, and even a country song for Mr. Yakov Smirnoff. He is a famous Russian comedian who had made it big in the United States using his communist experience as a comedy foil for democracy and, as a result, landed himself on The Tonight Show, a national commercial with Best Western Hotels, and Caesar's casino gigs in Las Vegas and Atlantic City. He also had a huge, beautiful house (Dom Delouise lived across the street, and Michael Keaton lived next door) at the Riverside Country Club in southern California.

I met him one night by accident at a fairly small lakeside casino in northern California. His original opening act had fallen ill that day, and I was asked to fill in for two shows on a Friday night in the summer of 1992. The producer had asked me to do a fifteen-minute comedy set and then bring up Mr. Smirnoff with a warm introduction. So that's exactly what I did.

Yakov was a little bit late for the first show, so I never actually met him until I said from the stage: "Thank you, ladies and gentlemen. I enjoyed my fifteen minutes of fame, and now I'd like to introduce your headliner, the man whose name you DID know, the comedy you actually bought a ticket for . . . Mr. Yakoff Smirnoff."

Yakov came strolling along the stage, a big old grin on his face. As he shook my hand, he whispered, "I just watched your set. I'm still laughing about a couple of jokes. Watch my set right now and give me some notes?"

Of course, I thought he was kidding. It turns out he wasn't. So I wrote four pages of punch lines, tag lines, and premise ideas for a funny millionaire.

In between the first and second show, he said, "Why don't you come to my dressing room. I want to talk to you about some work."

First Thought Wrong? Second thought wrong? Third thought wrong? I know he wants me to sleep with him, but what will I get out of it?

When we got there, he said: "I love your joke about the ex-wife, the plaintiff, and how she taught your four-year-old daughter about the value of money! Your ex-wife saying, 'Courtney, honey, pick up that nickel. There, money does not grow on trees! No, no. We get it in the mail from your daddy!' Ha ha ha. I like dat joke!"

He took a look at the pages I had brought in with me and noticed that there were several of them. A little embarrassed, he said to me: "This is a lot of notes. I did not realize I was this bad a comedian!" We both laughed at that.

After a couple of hours of reading the show notes I had made for him and discussing a few minor terms and details, we came to an arrangement where he would fly me down to the Hollywood area where he lived, and I would write with him for a whole week. Writing comedy for a very famous, professional, and funny man was truly an honor. And it turns out he really was funny. I learned that fact the first time he and I went to lunch together just the two of us.

It was an average Tuesday morning in Beverly Hills, California. Sunshine, luxury cars, exposed skin, lots of expensive jewelry, and high-end retail shops everywhere.

Yakov and I had reservations at a cool little café with a nice private table set aside so that we could talk about comedy strategy and a whole bunch of other things as we got to know each other; it was our first day as boss/employer and relatively unknown hired gun.

I was very excited, and I could not wait to absorb everything I was about to learn from a guy who was exactly where I wanted to be someday. He had a gift, and I had a gift. His gift had gotten him a whole bunch of things I already mentioned, as well as a beautiful wife, two beautiful kids, and a knowing, admiring glance from every single patron in that restaurant.

My gift had gotten me fired from Food Villa.

Remember that we were in Hollywood, where everybody is in show business. Everybody is in the movie and television entertainment industry in one form or another. Heck, the valet guy had a development deal with Paramount.

As Yakov and I sat there waiting for our server to grab us a couple of iced teas, he said, "I'm very happy to have you on board. I think your stuff is very funny. A few years from now, you may be too expensive for me to hire you as a writer."

I knew he was teasing me and buttering me up, but it felt good, and

I wanted to do my very best for him.

The waitress came by to take our order. "Are you two ready to order some lunch?"

Yakov: "No, no, no . . . Not just yet, dear. This is a working lunch for us, and we will be taking our time. Thank you."

The waitress took a beat, then pouted her lips and stalked away. I only noticed because I was kind of hungry and wanted to eat. But this was work. I had to learn some discipline and boundaries, I guess.

Minutes later, she came back:

"Gentlemen, are we ready to order?"

Yakov responded, "No, young lady, as I said, we're working. When we're ready to order our food, we will let you know. I will wave you over. Thank you."

The waitress turned without a word and stomped back into the kitchen. This time, I watched the entire interaction with a keen eye. I thought this might be funny at some point. One of the things you learn as a comedian or comedic writer is that everything funny has a single common denominator: conflict. I had a great comic lens for material. I was about to see some more.

Some minutes later, she came back. "OK, guys, let's get some food started for you. The lunch rush is about to happen. I actually have more than this one table and I don't wanna get behind. I make my living serving food, and I'd really like to turn this table a couple of times in the next couple of hours, know what I'm saying?"

Yakov curtly responded, "Young lady, I said I would wave you over when we are ready to order. I have not done that yet."

The waitress replied, "Look, I serve tables so I can pay rent, but I'll tell you something, mister, I'm actually an actress! That's right. An actress. And until I can make a living at that, I have to do this. Now do you understand?"

Yakov responded, "Wow, well, why didn't you say so? Are you a good actress?"

"Yes, I'm a very good actress!"

Yakov said, "Well then, why don't you act like a waitress and wait for us to call you over when we're ready to order?"

I remember doing a spit take right there with a mouth full of water that I wish

I'd held back. This job was already worth the money, and I hadn't even had my first meal.

But I did get a lesson that day. I wondered about the actress and how she had handcuffed herself in that situation.

Yakov had some juice in that town.

What if she had just done a great job during the waitress part of her life and he had been so impressed with her and her bubbly personality and amazing professional skills that he had inquired about the actress part of her life? I learned you never know who you're working with or for because they might be someone important! Or someone important soon.

Over and over and over and over, I learned that the gift I had needed to be applied in a way that would serve more than just Mark Lundholm. I tried for a few years to fit into a comedy mold, act like the right guy to get something I thought I wanted or needed, use the right words, and elicit the right response so I could feel right about doing comedy.

Yakov Smirnoff said to me, "You're sober? Yourself?"

"Yes," I said. He then said something to me that I can still remember verbatim: "Oh, well then . . . That's your thing. You're going to be the Recovery Guy. Everybody has a thing. I think that will be yours." And right he was.

OAKLAND DOPE DEALS

In the late 1970s and early '80s, I lived in the Oakland hills. A place called Montclair—a high-end residential neighborhood separated from Oakland by a narrow ribbon of road called the Warren Freeway.

Everything below the Warren was mid- to low-range expensive.

Everything above the Warren was beyond what you or I could afford. Ever.

Luckily for me at the time, I was renting a tiny apartment and sharing it with two other people. All of us were drug addicts and alcoholics, but none of us knew it at the time.

I actually remember thinking, "I hope this time lasts the rest of my life!"

The folks who lived in these hills and nearby Piedmont were celebrities, rockstars, and professional athletes. I was selling cocaine to a few of them, going to parties with some of them, and worshiping every one of them.

I was twenty-one years old. I was already in a life way over my head, but then again, I had that gift of gab. Remember? The one I told you about? I'd had it a long time, and during this period of my life, I used it like a rubber band: Stretch it out as far as it will go, hope that it holds and hope it doesn't snap back on me. For a while it almost worked out that way.

A few months after I found myself in Montclair, working at Roberts Food Market (another grocery store, of course!), I met Huey P. Newton, one of the original founders of the Black Panther Party.

He was an ex-prison inmate, political activist, PhD in something or other, and, for lack of a better word, a god in northern California.

I got to know this man over the next couple of years. He could've been governor of California in a heartbeat and easily a mayor, senator, or, hell, whatever else he wanted to be! This man was a force of nature. He had physical strength; he had cover model good looks and charisma that you could feel from fifty feet away.

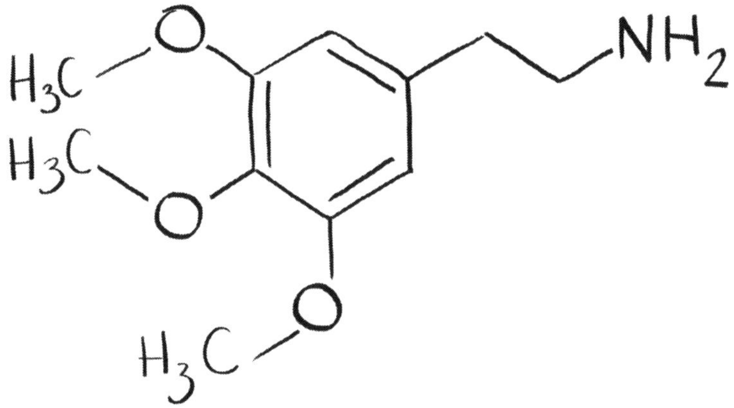

He also liked mescaline.

Cocaine and methamphetamine and any other upper were fine, but he liked mescaline.

There were many occasions when we were both at a party in the hills and I looked at him and thought, "I'll watch him from a distance, but if I get close to him I'm not safe."

There were lots of tough, powerful, wealthy people in the hills of Montclair. Most worked hard for their money and did something honest for a living.

I never saw a single one of them at any of our coke parties.

My dealer was a guy named Brian No Last Name. No Last Name because he's dead now. He got killed because he owed his dealer and could not pay him. Remember at the time I was twenty-one years old. And this all seemed pretty normal to me.

I have an incredible gift of being able to sense, smell, and even feel things about other people when I'm in their presence. I've had it my whole life. Still do. Back then, that gift wasn't so finely tuned, and I rarely used it to protect myself or anyone else I cared about. I was only interested in making money, doing dope, and feeling like I was in one of the important circles up in those damn hills.

After Brian was killed, I didn't bother to quit doing or selling dope. I simply found another dealer.

One Saturday night, very late, my brother David and I walked out of a bar called Crogan's on LaSalle Avenue. We only had about six blocks to go, heading to my tiny shared apartment, when I heard a couple of shoes scuffle on the sidewalk behind us.

Someone quickly stepped out from behind a tree near a chain-link fence and rushed up behind us. It was Huey.

"Don't move, coke man, or I'll pop your brother in the head."

I stopped in my tracks, slowly turned my head back over my shoulder, and saw that there was a gun pressed to the back of my brother's skull.

Mr. Huey P. Newton was holding a very large caliber weapon, and his hand was shaking. I can't tell you how scared I was. I just know that I've never felt like that since.

"Huey, Huey," I said, "We didn't do anything to you, man. You know me. What's going on, man? What's really going on here?"

"Give me that blow bag in your pocket or I'm gonna do him!" he replied.

I knew Newton would do just that. It was in his eyes. Those mescaline eyes. I said, "Yes, sir, I'm going to reach into my left pocket right now with my left hand. Real slow. And I'm going to toss you this bag. But Huey, I swear to God if you don't put that gun down, you're going to have to kill me and everybody I know. There are people up here that actually like me, man, remember? You used to be one of them. Remember Walnut Street?"

And I could see that he did.

At a party one night on Walnut Street, I had walked him out to his car. He hadn't remembered that he had a car there that night, but I had seen him pull up, park in the neighbor's driveway across the street, and stumble over to where the lights were all on and the people were all over the place. Party. That night, I dumped him into his car, stole his keys out of his pocket at the same time, called an Oakland police officer that I knew, and had them come rescue Huey (and his car keys) and take him home safely. Even some of the local PD idolized this guy. I'm not sure Huey ever knew it was me. But all of a sudden, I saw a tiny flicker of recognition in his eyes. He remembered.

I took out the bag of coke and flipped it in his direction. He picked it up, turned, and walked away without saying another word.

David started breathing again—I was still shaking like a leaf in December—and we both started trotting, then sprinting, toward my apartment.

I never spoke to or heard from Huey P. Newton again. I rarely thought about that night with David. Until I heard about Newton's death in 1989. Someone murdered him with a gun. By then, I no longer lived in the Oakland hills. I was in a halfway house in San Leandro, trying to stay sober and out of trouble. My first thought was, "What a waste. They killed the governor." Then I wept.

Chapter 9 Wrap-Up

These days, I'm quite convinced that if you have a gift, you have to give. Nobody has liabilities or shortcomings; we have only assets we are supposed to polish up so we can serve the universe. Give something big back by paying it forward.

Anything I used to use as weaponry could just as easily have been aimed at service to others or shelter for people I care about and the evolution of a truly informed, unselfish man. A man is like a new job and the universe that handed out those assets is the job site! And like the man said, "Do the job like you're trying to get the job."

Personal opinion here? If I want to complain, I really have to look for a reason to do it. The gifts I've received are immeasurable, and they keep coming. Friends, family, opportunity, personal growth, and satisfaction at work, etcetera etcetera. And, oh yeah, attention from the community, a significant reputation in an honorable industry, the ability to create comedy, make a difference in the lives of others, fresh air that's not recirculated stale jail breath, a phone with no time limit, food in the refrigerator that I chose and paid for, a bed that's comfortable in a home that's mine, and people I meet all day who are no threat to me. After looking at all those gifts and millions more, how could I not want to give something back to the universe that gave me everything I have? Once again, I go because I owe. You can quote me on this one: "When it comes to my attitude today, gifted and grateful beats victim and hateful every time."

Reflection Section:

Name one skill or talent you have that no one else in your family has.

What recent discovery have you made about yourself that involves shifting your lens from weapon to gift? From cursed to benefit?

What particular skill(s) are you using as a gift to the universe?

Chapter 10

The Argument You Win is the One You Don't Enter

Have you ever mistaken serenity for fatigue? I've always liked to debate, argue, and flat-out fight with people. Eventually, I would either run out of people to do those things with and end up incredibly lonely or become too exhausted to continue. Neither one of those places was where I wanted to be.

SAFEWAY SATURDAY

Grayson and I are huge hockey fans. Our team is the San Jose Sharks. We love the action, the pace, and the overall excitement and energy of an arena full of rabid hockey fans! We go to as many games as we can during the season. We also like to bring our own snacks! That's what we were doing in the Safeway store on this particular Saturday morning.

Grayson had grabbed a bag of Swedish Fish and a package of Sour Patch Kids. I went with my usual: Lemonheads and Cherry Sours. We would wait and buy the extra-large bag of salted peanuts when we got to the arena. Two root beers would top off the edible portion of our hockey experience that afternoon.

We took our stuff into the express lane at Safeway. We were way under the eleven-item minimum. Almost good to go now.

As we put our items down on the check stand's conveyor belt, I noticed someone standing behind me—way too close. Dysfunctional kids always have a spectacular sense of their proximity to humans or objects, a sort of antenna for safe sanctuary or comfortable distance from other people. I have a finely tuned bubble, a boundary around my own body that expands or contracts depending on my sense of safety in public. I've had it my whole life.

Whoever the person was behind me was definitely pushing on my bubble. I turned around.

She was a tiny, elderly woman. Very frail. I'm guessing ninety years old, eighty pounds, and barely five feet tall. She was about as harmless as a Q-tip in a knife fight. I giggled to myself just a little. I said, "Hello."

She looked up at me and said, "Hello. Would you mind handing me one of those long rubber bars right there? She indicated one of those nasty, filthy, germy separators that you put between people's groceries on the belt so you know whose things are whose. Because I'm a bit of a germaphobe, I never touch those things. Ever. Not ever. I said to the old woman, "Well, just push your stuff up and I'll pay for it."

"Oh, how nice of you," she said. "Thank you so much."

As I was paying attention to the old woman, some guy with just one item slipped right in front of me and budged the line to the express lane, handing his money to the cashier. No courtesy, no "Excuse me, sir." Not a mannerly word. Just stepped right in front of everyone. Right in front of me.

Grayson noticed and said, "Dad, that guy . . ."

"Yeah, G Money, I saw."

The guy turned around, looked at me, and said, "We got a problem here?"

First Thought Wrong. Second thought worse. Third thought: The jerk that cut the line had a ponytail. In a fight, that's a handle. Before this guy knows what's happening, I could hurt him as bad as I want as quickly as I could. But . . . I don't want to go to jail. I just want to go to a hockey game with my son. No need to turn this into an UnSafeway store.

I said, "No, no problem here."

The line-cutting guy said, "Yeah, I didn't think so."

In my brain, I could hear a growling tiger with teeth bared and a fully clawed paw ready to pull this guy's jaw off of his skull with one swipe.

First thought second thought third thought . . . My boy is at my hip, and I just want to go to the Sharks game. Slow your roll, Mark.

Grayson watched this whole interaction, looked up at me, and asked, "Dad? Are you mad? You look mad. I heard you breathe really loud. When you breathe really loud, I know you're mad."

Now, I wanted to tell my son the truth, but I had to be careful with the words I used.

Grayson had heard curse words, but they sounded different at our house. We say things like "son of a business major." Things like "cheese and rice" and "what the fudge brownie" and "holy shitake mushroom!" Those are bad words at our house, and we have to ask permission to use them. Especially Grayson. Permission.

So, sure enough, that's what my son does: "Dad, you did good just now not saying anything when you were mad. But can I use a bad word for a minute?"

I continued to breathe, slow down my thinking, get a cooler handle on things. The guy in front of me had finished his transaction and was now gone. I rubbed the top of my son's head and said, "Sure, buddy, you can use a bad word."

Grayson said, "That guy was a DICK!"

It stopped me dead in my tracks and made me giggle. Until I remembered the old lady standing right behind me. I slowly turned to look at her and said, "I'm sorry you had to hear that, ma'am."

Without blinking, without hesitation, she said, "That's OK. He was a dick!"

Staying out of an argument with that guy not only saved time, stress, and energy; it probably kept me out of jail or the hospital. And my boy and I got to the game! First Thought Wrong became Next Right Thing. Again.

FIRE DANGER THERMOMETER THEORY

When I say that what you think about most today is your guide, I'm 100 percent certain that that is true. I've proven it to myself for over twenty-five years now.

Here's how: Every morning when I wake up, I've got a chance of a solid, beneficial, healthy day. Unless I don't want that to be the case. You see, when I come to in the morning, I'm like that sign on the side of the highway that warns the driver about the fire danger on the road today. You know that sign that says, "Fire danger today. Low/moderate/high/danger"? There is a large arrow or needle on a board that goes from left to right, and the colors there represent the severity of the fire danger: Green is low, yellow is moderate, orange is high, and red is danger.

I have the same emotional arrow on a board, the same color designated arrangement for my emotional rating. And I've been sober long enough and I'm chronologically old enough to be able to read my boards and tell where the emotional fire danger is on a regular, consistent, and accurate basis—FIRST thing in the morning.

And I can continue to read the danger signs or feel the heat as I continue throughout my day.

I can actually take a random reading or check the board anytime I want throughout the day.

Call it what you will: Taking your own inventory, checking your temperature, what's your princess potential? How hot is the furnace?

As long as I get a regular reading on the thermometer during the day, I know what I'm thinking about most and what my guide has become for that day.

Back in the old days, pre-recovery, my guides during the day would have been things like cocaine, rage, punishment, debt, loss, poker, alcohol, pride, greed, fear, self-loathing, abuse, and criminality.

These days, my guide is her. She is a gentle wind, subtle and fearless, strong and loving, honest and kind and maternal.

Do you ever notice how you can't really see the wind? You can, however, see what it does, how it affects you and others, how strong it can be, the direction it takes us, and the fact that it is always present. Always.

Fire consumes! An argument does exactly the same thing: It burns up time and delays the truth from showing up. So, whenever I can, I like to work away from the heat and destruction of the fire with a strong but gentle wind at my back.

OATMEAL OR LUNCH?

Since the day my son Grayson was born, I realized there would come a time when we would be mano a mano. You can't have two males living under the same roof without some kind of contest, competition, or conflict.

I grew up in a house of five males. It was a war zone at times. Other times the best we could do was a two-hour truce. But there was always that knuckle-dragging Simian male creature simmering underneath. We loved each other the best we knew how, but we fought each other hard almost every day.

And now I have a son. Grayson Cole Lundholm. And he's been a sharp one since the day he arrived. Ferocious and smart and worldly and impatient. Did I mention ferocious? Like his mom and dad, Grayson can ramp up when it's his turn to talk or share an emotion. Like anger. I remember when he was in his terrible twos.

Julee and I wanted to go out for dinner, so we had gotten a sitter for Grayson. Her name was Patty, a family friend. Grayson really liked her, and he was always excited to see her when she came to babysit. It was a Saturday night, and Julee and I had not been out to dinner or alone on a date for quite some time. We were really looking forward to going out. All the time knowing he was in good hands.

When Patty knocked on the front door, Grayson and Julee were sitting on the couch in the living room. Patty walked in with her usual bubbly, loquacious, happy, upbeat self, and Grayson started to cry. He was at that age where everything that Mom and Dad wanted to do was the other side of the coin for him. He was going to make a statement that he didn't want Mom and Dad to go on a date, and he didn't want us to leave him there with Patty. Why? Why you ask?

Because he was two years old.

I closed the door, gave Patty a hug, and looked at Grayson's mom. Mama was just shaking her head slowly like, "Wow! He's never pulled this one before."

I said to Grayson, "Hey, buddy, slow down there. Look at me, son. It's OK. It's OK, G-man. Patty is here, and she's going to stay with you until we get back."

Grayson shouted, "No!"

"Hey, buddy, hey, buddy; yes."

Grayson: "No! Noooooo!"

Patty was stunned, and Julee looked at me like, "What are we gonna do?"

I leaned in close to Grayson and took one of his hands. I said, "Listen, Grayson. Mama and I are going out to dinner and Patty is going to watch you. And if you say no to me again, I'm going to slap your hand."

I saw fear in his eyes and some confusion. I had never hit him before. He said, "No!"

It was louder than the first three times put together. I slapped his hand as hard as I could.

He took one of those long inhaling breaths that seemed like it would never end.

We all knew that when he finally cried it was going to be a bellow and would probably be heard by the neighbors.

And that's exactly what it was. He was crying so hard it broke my heart, and it was contagious. Julee and Patty were both crying, and I had no idea what to do. I was in charge of the situation and I had to come up with a solution.

This also meant that my son wasn't going to win the argument.

I looked him dead in the eye, and I said, "Mom and I are going to dinner, and if you say no to me again I'm gonna hit your hand again."

With no words and no hesitation whatsoever, he stuck his arm straight up, putting his hand right in front of me, daring me to hit him.

The scene was so familiar to me I couldn't take it.

I remember exhaling, standing up, kissing him and my wife and Patty on their heads, then turning away, walking down the hall and into the master bedroom. I sat on the bed and began to sob. If I wasn't careful, my kid would grow up to be just like me. Hating authority, rebellious, and absolutely fearless about consequences. I was crying because I knew all of this was possible if I didn't change my way of teaching that boy.

A few minutes later, Julee came into the bedroom and sat down beside me. She told me that Patty had things under control and it would be OK for us to go to dinner.

"How are you feeling, big fella?" she asked.

I told her I didn't want to talk about it right then, so let's just get out of the house while we still can. We both laughed a little at that and headed for the car.

I never hit Grayson again. I've never even had the need to hit him again. I made a promise to myself, to Julee, and to my son that I would never put myself in that position ever again. I never wanted to be stuck in a place where the only thing left to do was hit the kid.

Sometime later, Julee said something to me that I'll never forget. "Remember that night you smacked our son's hand? Remember how out of control that situation seemed? He was only two years old! What the £*#% was our excuse?"

A year or two later, Grayson and I were in the kitchen at breakfast time. I said to my son, "Hey, buddy, are you ready for your oatmeal?"

Grayson answered, "Dad, I want pancakes for breakfast."

"Well, it's oatmeal for breakfast today, buddy."

Grayson whined, "Dad, I don't want oatmeal; I said I want pancakes."

"Well, you're the boss. You can have oatmeal for breakfast, or you can wait till lunch to eat. Oatmeal breakfast now or you can eat lunch in four hours."

Grayson replied dramatically, "OK, OK. Oatmeal, please."

"Good choice, captain," I said.

It had taken me a while, but I had learned the secret. No argument, no slap, no threat of either one was as effective as two solutions that would remedy the situation, and I could live with either choice. Win-win . . . win.

Chapter 10 Wrap-Up

This realization was one of the greatest moments of clarity I've had in my entire life. I actually pierced the veil of dysfunctional family history and saw that I had a choice about whether to give someone a beating or send him a simpler message; whether to stand and fight or stand up and lead; whether to take a punch or take a pass on the entire event. It was eye-opening for me.

Where I aim my attention, intelligence, and gifts are my choice, not a decision I ever need to let someone else make for me. When it comes to recovery, I'm involved or I'm invisible. I'm in truth or I'm in trouble. I'm in recovery or I'm in relapse. I'm whiny or I'm shiny! I'm the exception to a healthy direction or I'm exceptional because of it. Oh, man! There's a whole bunch of power running through me right now as I say that, write that, read that, and remember that.

Reflection Section:

Where or when can you recall not backing down in an argument and regretting it?

Have you been in a situation recently where you avoided confrontation and did not feel like you lost respect or status or leverage in the process?

Is there a current challenge or conflict in your life today that would be managed better by avoiding an argument?

Chapter 11

#BEFIRST. If You Don't See Some, Be Some

Waiting around for someone to hand me power, freedom, equality, grace, or strength was why I spent a ton of time wandering around lost. Eventually, I got tired of looking for PERMISSION to be better.

THE PRODUCER OF SHOWTIME

In the late '90s, I could pretty much headline at any comedy club in the country. I had great relationships with the big chains and the really big independents. Comedy clubs were popular and viable but not thriving like they were in the late '80s. I still enjoyed the work, with live, close, intimate settings and solid venues that knew what the heck they were doing when it came to production.

But the road itself was starting to wear on me. It was making me tired and grumpy and a little jaded about humanity.

My mood was almost perfect for a TV special. Hollywood in general, and the comedy industry in total, LOVE bitter and edgy and critical and hard. I got my chance.

Cobb's Comedy Club was one of San Francisco's most venerable and respected entertainment venues. Tom Sawyer was the owner, and I had become very fond of him and his staff and his wonderful club.

Everyone you have ever heard of in standup comedy worked for Tom at one time or another.

I was living in San Jose, California, and San Francisco was just a short drive north from my apartment. Three or four times a year, I would do a two- or three-night stint at Cobb's. The pay was decent, the crowds were bright, and my opening acts were always pretty fair comedians. I could work out new material, experiment, and take risks with jokes or stories that I would eventually fine-tune for the rest of my shows or talks around the country.

At this point in my career, I was also doing a ton of work with recovery crowds and mental health professionals at conventions, conferences, and keynote speeches. About seventy-five percent of my work in the year 2000 had become recovery-specific or based on the mental health profession's needs for humor and education. I had developed a niche.

One Tuesday morning, I received a call from Tom Sawyer. I was asleep, so he left a message asking me to call him back. I did: "Hey, boss, what's shakin' up there?"

Tom said, "Good news, my young friend. I've got a showcase I want you to do. It's for *Showtime*. They've got a nationwide search in five or six major cities, looking for some new talent in the US. Boston, New York, Minneapolis, San Francisco, LA, Seattle, and I think Denver. Anyway, they wanted me to put together a list of twenty comedians. I thought you might be interested."

"Sure, Tom. If you think I should."

Tom said, "Don't be an idiot." And he was gone.

My previous experience with standup comedy on television had been . . . well, watching other comedians on television. I had never done the *Tonight Show* or *Letterman* or any other late-night sites where comedians could get noticed. I had been grinding it out on the road for the better part of ten years. I had performed in every state in the United States and four foreign countries. I had done shows in hundreds of prisons, treatment centers, military bases, hospitals, shelters, and jails. I had worked on cruise ships, in small theaters, and at colleges and community centers. But I had never performed on TV.

I was excited to audition but nervous about what I had to offer a mainstream network or producer. Looking back, I smile when I think of how naive that statement was and how much I underestimated my material. I had consistently entertained individuals in crowds in some of the harshest, most undesirable venues you could present to any comedian. And I was thriving. But what the hell could I do for a regular audience?

For the audition, there were ten comedians on Friday night and ten more on Saturday evening. I was a Friday guy. I knew a few of the other comedians, and I assumed that all twenty entrants in the showcase would be formidable.

We were all told that the Showtime producer would only select one of us.

When I heard that, I knew that I had no chance. I wasn't as funny as some of them, but I knew for a fact that I was not funnier than any of them.

I worked on my setlist for two weeks and decided I would pick the funniest stuff I had and run with that. The set was supposed to be ten minutes long and represent what each of us could do comedically; our point of view, so to speak. I wasn't even sure I had a point of view. But I definitely had some original stuff that made people laugh.

I put together my ten-minute set and practiced it until I was sick of the words coming out of my mouth. Two days before the showcase, I had memorized every word, blink, breath, and physical gesture I needed to do a solid performance for the *Showtime* guy.

Thursday morning, the day before what I considered the biggest performance of my comedy career, I had a thought: What am I not seeing? I'm missing something.

I woke up that morning, and a gut hunch nagged at me. It was a powerful voice, a firm whisper saying, "You have something they don't." I wasn't sure what it meant, so I thought about it over breakfast. I went to my favorite little deli in San Jose—Gunthers! It had become like a second office for me. I always sat at the same table and pretty much ate the same food. They always served me my favorite drink: hot, black coffee with a shot of espresso. I was sipping out of my coffee mug when it hit me like a freight train. I needed to change my setlist!

I can't describe the panic that went through me in that instant. I had memorized my ten solid minutes of original comedy. But after reading through the list one more time, I realized that it didn't say very much about me or my point of view or anything different from anyone else who would take the stage this weekend. I needed to start over, even though it was the day before I would appear before a *Showtime* network executive. Fine. No pressure at all. I went back to the drawing board.

I put together ten of the most unique minutes that Ken Weinstock, the Showtime producer, would see in ANY city where he held a showcase. I decided that I had to sell out the big laughs for the bigger picture. So I put together a list of the darkest, most aggressive, hard-to-look-at stories that I had lived through during my addiction.

My gut was telling me that this was right and that these experiences were going to be useful. My head was telling me, "What the #&*$ do you think you're doing?" but my gut won the argument. By Thursday night, I had crafted a brutally honest set, absolutely original in its storytelling elements and 100 percent true. It contained a whole bunch of laughs and not one single punchline. I knew it would be different than anything I had ever done for public viewing. It was a veiled recovery show, standup comedy with a sober compass. I began to put it to memory, and I didn't sleep that night.

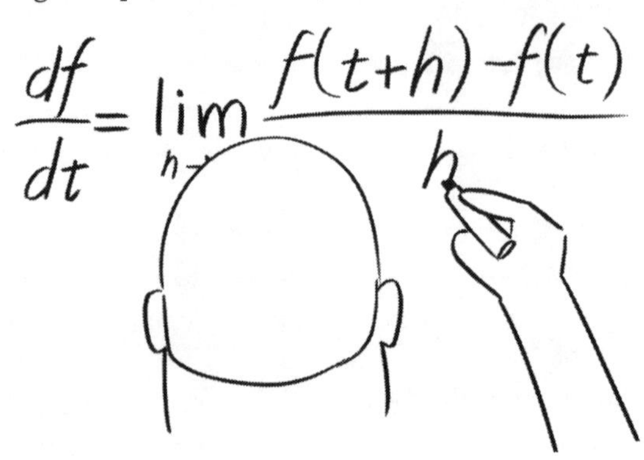

Friday night, I went to Cobb's Comedy Club. I was eighth out of ten that night in the rotation. My set destroyed the audience. And impressed one of the producers. I had done it!

Mr. Weinstock watched the last two comedians that night, walked to the back of the room where I was sitting on a barstool watching the night progress, took out a piece of paper, and said to me, "How would you like to do a thirty-minute special on *Showtime*?"

I took a beat, looked over at the other nine comedians who had gathered in a group, raised my eyes to meet the man's face, and said, "Can I check my calendar?" And we both started laughing.

In 2001, I recorded my first TV special for the Showtime comedy network. It was funny and original and showcased all the things I had to offer as a recovering person who had survived a dysfunctional family, jail, the street, rehab, mental illness, and the abusive, early lifestyle of a road comic. The decision to pick material that was absolutely and totally mine, that wouldn't be repeated no matter how many comedians Showtime looked at that year, was one of the single best career decisions I've ever made. But it sure wasn't my FIRST thought.

SIOUX FALLS AA

Nitwits Comedy Club. A Sioux Falls, South Dakota landmark. It was located in the basement of a brewery. No kidding. I was doing a full week there as the headliner, and I was exhausted. I had been on the road for five weeks and had traveled all over the Midwest. Tulsa, Omaha, Chicago, Dallas. I was run down physically and emotionally drained to the very bottom of my tank.

Never a good place for a recovering alcoholic and even worse for a dysfunctional, self-centered, recovering addict. I happen to be both, and on this particular weekend I was in bad shape.

Every so often, the universe reminds me that sober doesn't mean sane, and clean does not mean cured. I have to step up at times and take care of myself when the world doesn't seem to want to do that for me. I know, I know. Adults should know that by now, right? Sometimes I have selective memory loss when it comes to the healthy stuff. I have a tendency to run myself ragged pursuing a passion and then conveniently wonder why I don't have the energy to be productive anymore. Wow.

I called the central office hotline for the Sioux Falls twelve-step community. I was told that there was a Sunday morning meeting on a piece of Native American land about twenty minutes outside of Sioux Falls. The meetings started at 9 a.m. and ran for a full hour. I asked the volunteer on the hotline if she had ever been to the meeting, and she said she had not, but she heard that the guy running the meeting was a long-time member and very reliable.

I thought, "Well, what the heck?" I really need a meeting, and Native American land (which is really the entire United States if you think about it) has always been a safe and calming influence on Mark Lundholm. So I decided I would get up early on Sunday, have a small breakfast, grab a huge cuppa coffee, and steer my cheap little rental car in the direction of something healthy: a twelve-step meeting. Which has also always been a safe and calming influence on Mark Lundholm.

I was surprised that I only got lost one time along the way.

Though I have a gift for reading people and an uncanny internal sense of time, my sense of direction is atrocious. An exercise in humility for me used to be trying to read a map and get someplace without planning in an extra hour or two of "getting lost" time.

I did the best I could, and I got to the meeting five minutes early. I considered this a small victory and a good way to start a Sunday. I saw the sign that said "9 a.m. AA" and walked through the door of a vast hall. I was a little surprised at what I saw next.

Inside the assembly hall, about twenty-five chairs were facing an eight-foot table with two more chairs behind it. Along one of the walls, there was a huge coffee urn, paper cups, sugar, creamer, and a box of donuts. There were individual little tin ashtrays that you could pick up and take to your chair while you smoked during the meeting.

This was in the mid-eighties, and almost every meeting in the world was a smoking meeting. I used to do a joke about it: "In AA meetings, there are two seating sections: smoking and lying about quitting."

I noticed this meeting had just about everything you needed—except people. One man was sitting in one of the chairs at the table. He was wide, old, ponytailed, and stoic. He looked almost like a statue, but I approached him knowing that if he was the secretary, he would be able to tell me what was going on. It was now 8:59 a.m.

"Morning, brother," I greeted him. "I'm looking for the meeting, and I think I'm in the right place, yeah?"

"That you are, young blood, that you are. I'm Steve."

"Mark," I replied.

He stood up, and we shook hands. Then he offered me the chair next to him at the table. This surprised me because, in most twelve-step settings, the other chair at the lead table is reserved for the speaker that day. I was just there to attend as a regular anonymous member.

I took the chair that was offered and sat down in it. He said, "I guess we'll get started then. How it works. Rarely have we seen a person fail."

I was amazed and a little impressed. He and I were the only ones in the meeting. But he was going ahead with the procedure and the format and the message as if he hadn't noticed how alone we were. It was a pretty good focus on his part. It made me feel more comfortable about being the center of attention for only one other human being.

Makes me giggle now even thinking about it.

As is the usual custom after the readings are done, he introduced me as "Mark, a member who will be sharing his story today."

I started talking about myself and was just going along for the ride, following Steve's directions. After a few minutes of talking, I don't think either one of us cared that we were the only ones in the room. We had chairs, a pot of coffee, and something in common. Hell, I even started to feel good about it just being us. It was odd, but it wasn't bad. Still, I couldn't help being curious about why no one else was attending this meeting.

Steve was about to explain it to me.

I finished my story and thanked Steve for calling on me and inviting me to share.

He spoke for a little while about his own story, where he had come from, where he had been, what he had changed, and what life was like for him right now. Steve had a great story and an even greater willingness to recover and stay sober. He'd been in AA for over twenty years. For a guy like me with six or seven years sober, twenty years was an eternity. He was already at the icon level and immediately was granted superstar status by me! Twenty years! Impressive.

We closed up the meeting in the usual manner, and I stood up from the table to say goodbye.

"Steve," I said, "Thanks for letting me lead the meeting, although it didn't seem like you had many options today. Where is everyone? I have never been to a meeting with just two people before."

"Oh, it's always like this. I've been doing this meeting for almost a year now. I guess I'm used to it, but it probably looked a little weird to you when you walked in, huh?"

"Weird?" I replied, "I thought I was in the wrong place or I set my watch ahead by an hour by accident. My first thought was to turn around and leave without asking any questions. But I'm glad I didn't. It was kind of cool in here, you know, just us, but I have to ask you: How many people usually come to this meeting?"

"Actually . . . you are the very first one," Steve replied.

"Huh? The first one today?" I asked.

Steve answered, "Besides me, you're the first one ever."

"You mean to tell me that you've been doing this meeting for a whole year. By yourself. Every Sunday. For a whole year?"

"Yeah. One year. A whole year. Just me."

"Man," I replied, "I've heard of dedicated service, but why would you do that? Why would you keep showing up, making coffee, putting out the chairs?"

Steve answered: "I knew someone would show up eventually. Turns out it was you. Now you gotta do it for the next guy."

To this day, I think about him a lot. Occasionally, some detoxing newcomer will ask me, "Why do you do this? Why do you come here? You've been sober so long, why do you come and talk to us rookies?"

I usually answer, "Lots of reasons. I want to help. I've been given a lot, and I need to give something back. Sometimes it's selfish because I get something out of this as well. But one of the biggest reasons I can think of? Because Steve did it for me."

The newcomer will inevitably ask, "Who is Steve?" And I'll get to tell the story again.

THE MOST IMPORTANT PERSON

How do YOU get from one place to another? What kind of scooter or bicycle do you ride? What kind of car do you own? Are you a truck driver? Do you travel in a Prius, a Benz, a VW, a Chevy, a Subaru?

OK, I have a question for all of you: The day you got that vehicle or transportation device, what kind of car or truck or bike did you start noticing a whole BUNCH of all of a sudden? Right, YOURS! Do you think that the new vision of sameness was something the universe delivered to you only on that day? Don't you know that the world looks different to you because you have recently changed your lens?

You now had Jaguar eyes or Ford F-150 eyes or BMW eyes or Jeep eyes.

Every day, the mirror we look into is the rest of the world. Chances are that if you spot it, you brought it. People we see are usually a reflection of the person we are. If you leave the house feeling a certain way or possessing a certain mindset, experience has shown that you will see plenty of evidence to support whatever your emotion or attitude is that day.

What if we made it work for us the other way around? How much more empowered would you feel if you left the house today feeling bold and faithful and competent and worthy? And all day, you noticed evidence in support of those things when you looked at the world or into the faces of other human beings? You spot some because you brought some!

One of my daily rituals in the morning is #BEFIRST. Peace, patience, understanding, humor, grace, forgiveness, and gratitude. If I don't see some out there, I will be some out there. I am the most important person in my life today. Not in a self-centered way, but in the way of a centered self. I am responsible for my primary care.

I've discovered that if I am the most important person in Mark's life, Mark can make room for more persons in Mark's life. With integrity. And I can be authentic about telling people that I care for them because I know what care from me feels like. If we truly treated ourselves like people we love—respectfully, warmly, healthily, lovingly—how much better off would we be? Spiritually. Physically. Emotionally. Psychologically. TOTALLY!

#BEFIRST . . . Imagine. What if the world could do that? If every person you met today was the most important person in the world today, including you, what would the world be like today? Everyone wins. Nobody would lose. Nobody would even come in second. Every day, every human would win the human race. We'd get to bed safe and fed, leading by example the entire way!

I used to get caught in the vortex of "love you, lose me." This meant that in order to connect to something or someone I loved, I had to give up caring for myself. Like becoming invisible was the ultimate sacrifice. Then I found recovery and the real truth. I had been using the word "love" instead of "want," "need," "use," or "serve" (all in the most negative sense). I've discovered that being the most important person in my life can turn "Love you, lose me" into "Love me, include you" as I care for all parties involved, and nobody becomes less than.

Reflection Section

In what ways can you lead today instead of following the standard course?

What current situation in your life is unsatisfactory to you? And what will be the first action you take to do something about it?

Can you recall a time in your recent past when your input, change, focus, or energy immediately made all the difference in the world?

Epilogue

Thank you for reading this book. I am grateful to you and the many people who have helped me in this process. In the most humble fashion I can manage, I hope that something in your world has been made simpler, more clear. And as a result, you've been given another option or two that will allow you and the people you care about to heal, evolve, grow, forgive, and thrive.

Remember that nothing in life is accidental and that your passion and purpose and path are unique and wonderful. This world would be missing something necessary and valuable if you weren't here. You are a piece of a jigsaw puzzle, a patch in the quilt, a lyric line in a song this world sings to the universe. Enjoy your amazing existence. Celebrate your worth.

You've earned a very special place in your own life.

Oh, and one other thing. Don't let other people tell you what to do!

Mark Lundholm and his daughter, Courtney

Mark Lundholm and First Lady Betty Ford

Mark Lundholm on stage

Mark Lundholm, Grayson, and Julee

About Wholehearted Publishing

Life is filled with challenges and opportunities. For many of us, it can take decades to begin to understand ourselves and the world around us. Our books and programs are developed to save you time and reduce suffering by encouraging personal growth, self-understanding, and awareness through quality content. Wholehearted Thought Leaders and authors embody wisdom, philosophy, and practical skills that can help you gain focus, clarity, growth, healing, and most importantly, self-compassion.

Other Books & Audiobooks You Might Like

What if You're Not as Fucked up as You Think You Are?
by Dr. Adriana Popescu

Conscious Recovery
Conscious Being
Conscious Creation
by TJ Woodward

Enough Already!
A Guide to Recovery from Alcohol and Drug Addiction, and Get Your Life Back! by Bob Tyler

Made in the USA
Middletown, DE
21 September 2024